Legendary Selling For The 21st Century

The Guide to Exceeding Your Own Expectations

-Terrie Anderson-

999 LEGENDARY SELLING FOR THE 21ST CENTURY

© Copyright Terrie Anderson December 2009

First Edition Printed March, 2010

All Rights Reserved

No part of this book may be reproduced in anyway, or by any means, without permission in writing of the publisher.

Any characters or organisations referred to in this book have their names changed to protect their identity.

Published By Easy Online Portals Pty Ltd

GPO Box 865

Brisbane 4001 Australia

Contact Us at terrie.anderson@easyonlineportals.com

Cover Design Rudy Pauwels

ISBN 978-0-9807248-3-7

What Is In This For You?

999 Legendary Selling for the 21st Century is unique.

It is for those sales people who are already accomplished in the basic techniques of selling, but who yearn to reach the top of their profession, or make millions, or even to become a Legend.

When you become a 999er, you have all the information you need to fly like an eagle!

999 is not for the feint hearted, the lazy or the contented. It is for professional sales executives who are prepared to commit to a holistic approach, honestly review their habits and make change where necessary.

A Sales Legend does not cruise, they are on fire!

A fire fed with endless self-generated energy and filled with a sense of wanting more. More recognition, more sales, or more money. There is no evil in wanting more, do you know any wealthy, successful person who wants any less?

Sales people with ambition, should beware of contentment. Whilst it may give you a certain sense of serenity, it is the enemy of abundance. Contentment will breed boredom in an intelligent person, and eventually cause heartache. You will achieve for a few years, then fall into periods of restlessness, uncertain about what you want or how to bring the energy back. Often called burn out.

Sales Legends do not burn out, they feed their fire daily.

They know how to take intelligent breaks, motivate themselves and others, and most importantly achieve a daily lifestyle balance.

For some people contentment works, they want a chilled life, and that is ok, unless you want to be a Sales Legend.

We will revisit some things you may already know. I want you to check you still do them. We will also repeat important messages in different chapters to demonstrate how each skill is a habit, and each habit is interwoven through strategy, planning and execution of an unbeatable sales campaign. Sometimes it is something so small that prevents someone from greatness.

999 is a holistic coaching program, not a sales course. I am going to ask you to change some habits and this will extend right across your life. However, the rewards will also extend out and help you achieve a quality of life that can prevent burnout.

There are new elements, applicable to the changing environment of the 21st Century. There are things that have always been important to high achievers. There will even be some secrets, that collectively unlock the code of success (they explain magic that some people have) but they may challenge your reality.

Hard truth says a sales person is as valuable as their last three wins! 999 helps you achieve consistency, and repetition, of wins.

If you embrace the coaching in 999 Legendary Selling For The 21st Century, and introduce all the elements we discuss that are not already part of your daily life, then **you will increase your results**.

You may even become a Sales Legend!

INDEX

5	Overview
21	Integrity
41	Human Connection
107	Political Reference
129	Hard Line Qualification
145	Focus
159	Follow Up
173	Strategy
195	The Consortium
201	Customer Enthusiasm
235	Networking and Reputation
251	Art of Replication
259	What Now?
283	More Information
287	Contact Us

About Terrie Anderson

"A Sales Legend does not cruise they are on fire!"

Terrie Anderson has spent more than twenty years studying, speaking and coaching in legendary selling, motivation of high performance teams, and human empowerment whilst enjoying a very successful sales career. She has worked in Senior Sales Leadership roles for some of the top companies in IT Software, Hardware and Services; Telecommunications; Manufacturing and Fast Moving Consumer Goods. Terrie has demonstrated an outstanding track record of achievement and success in her career, and has a particular passion for complex solution selling.

Terrie is a recognised authority in the areas of sales, leadership, strategy, change management and a specialist in new business and turnarounds. Terrie has repeatedly built high performance teams by motivating the people to achieve their best willingly and happily.

She is also the author of 30 Days of Inspiration, The Little Red Success Book and many articles on success, leadership and motivation. Reaching senior level management in an international corporation by age of 28, she attained Board level positions just a few years later.

She is a dynamic and passionate speaker and recognised globally for motivating sales people to over achieve.

She approaches the world with warmth, happiness and an open honesty that has won her considerable esteem. Terrie is totally committed to the practices, and philosophies, outlined in her books and continues to live them as part of her daily life.

Raised in the Australian outback, she has travelled the world visiting many remote places and meeting people from many cultures. She has lived and worked internationally for many years, whilst holding strong ties to her native Australia.

Terrie is presently living between Europe and Australia with her personal and business partner, and their treasured friend Easydog.

She continues to promote the concept of health and happiness through success and sheer joy of life.

Terrie can be contacted:

By email   terrie.anderson@easyonlineportals.com

Testimonials for Terrie Anderson

Read what others who have worked with Terrie directly have to say about her:

"Terrie impressed me as direct, commercial, and clear thinking, as well as capable of getting things done in a difficult environment. A pleasure to deal with. Great skills for today's environment..."

"Terrie is someone who always gives you her time, and makes sure that that time is as productive as possible. Hugely respected not only across continental Europe, but further afield, she is highly influential and as a minor aside, is a lovely person to boot!"

"Terrie combines excellent sales management skills on both an operational and strategic level with exceptional people management skills. Her clear vision, strategy and communication skills allowed her to improve both the sales and services organizations. Terrie is the most effective business executive I have ever worked for"

"Terrie is one of a select few executive managers that excel at communication and at the same time possess very strong business acumen. It was a great pleasure to work with her."

Terrie has an incredible ability to get people motivated and get things happening. I recommend her highly."

"Terrie is just great to work with! She's straightforward, understands immediately what you want, to do business and just makes it happen with no complications."

"Terrie combines key skills : highly effective operational sales-skills; excellent executive and people –rapport; creative and magnetic in working solutions at all levels. Terrie's end-to-end understanding of business, based on significant personal track-record , make her an invaluable and highly credible business partner for getting "things done", sales, operations and people."

Terrie is a world-class sales executive with extensive experience in both Europe as well as Asia/Pacific. Highly recommended."

'Her superb leadership skills, sharp wit, and enormous business acumen are an invaluable asset to any company.

"Terrie was one of the most inspiring bosses that I've ever had, my only regret is that we didn't work together for longer. Terrie also gave me a great interest in working with people across cultures, as Terrie is one of the most intuitive people I have ever met

You are welcome to view the full Professional Bio for Terrie Anderson on

http://be.linkedin.com/in/terrieanderson

Overview

There are many sales people out there, similarly there are many actors out there, what they share in common is that only a very few make it to the top.

Sales Legends are not born. They are not made. They develop from the results and actions of people with the talent, who have the passion and the commitment to learn. They have the tenacity to apply what they have learnt intelligently in the field. They sweat in training, actively seek out and adopt mentors, and then motivate themselves to keep practising until they truly excel at their profession.

Why are there so few?

I challenge that it is because many will settle for 'good enough' and believe that to earn more money, they would have to work much harder, give up lifestyle or do things that are unethical. Some even change companies to get lower targets. In my many years of sales leadership experience, 'good enough' seems to be interpreted as somewhere between 85 and 110% of target achieved every quota period.

The problem is, too many of you are sitting out there in your comfort zone, happy enough with 'good enough'. Yet if I could reach out and touch you with the magic wand of motivation, you may amaze yourself. You could exceed all your own expectations, you just have to make the commitment to excellence, and follow through with the elements in this guide.

To be an average achiever is absolutely OK if that is good enough for you. I firmly believe that to be happy in life, many of us only need to meet our own expectations. The world needs you too! With average results most of you will retain your jobs and have decent lifestyles and maybe that is enough for you.

However, I meet many sales people out there who want to know how to achieve much more. They have more than just hunger. Hungry people when fed, may rest feeling satiated. These potential 999ers are restless, and need always to be moving toward lofty goals to satisfy their own needs for achievement and recognition.

It is entirely possible, although probably hard to believe, that by working smarter, applying oneself with greater commitment and lighting the fire of passion it is possible to significantly increase your success, and therefore your income. You do not need to give up your life, your family and have no time for yourself. You don't actually have to work longer hours, you may even be able to work less hours and have more quality time for your family, friends and hobbies.

Comfort Zones are a dangerous place for sales people, and even more devastating for the companies that allow them to flourish. Again, I challenge you when I say that in many organizations sales targets are set too low, or Sales Leaders are too tolerant when they accept repeated performances below 100%.

I want to share with you a recent example of a Comfort Zone that bothers me so much it interrupts my sleep whilst writing this guide.

> *Recently, a colleague of mine moved from the UK to Australia with his family and a fabulous new role. After arrival, he used the internet to specify the requirements for the new cars for his family. Then he sent his nearest dealer an email enquiry, and asked for a quotation for two vehicles to be supplied. After a few days, my colleague had received no response.*

He then wrote another email requesting a quotation and sent it to five branded dealers, commenting that the first person to get back to him would get the business.

Incidentally, it is interesting to mention here that the order value was approximately quarter of a million dollars worth of motor vehicles, and he had already selected not only brand but full specifications. This was a 'bluebird', the awesome opportunity that comes only a few times in a sales persons' career.

The outcome was that only one of the five sales people ever bothered to respond to his request. They sent the quote, they received the order.

As a result that person won Salesperson of The Month!

It is my belief the sales quotas in those dealerships are way too low!

Obviously, most of these sales people earn enough to be comfortable and fed. The Sales Leaders and Management are not driving a passion for excellence, they are not setting a competitive environment where sales people begin to unfold into their true potential. The dealerships are therefore less likely to attract and retain high achievers.

You see again my original analogy between actors and sales people. Very few will demonstrate passion and be recognised, and even fewer will become legends. A legend would be hunting every second of his or her work day for additional opportunity, and have their bluebird net poised for catching. They would never fail to check their emails!

This guide is about what differentiates a Sales Legend from a Good

Sales Person. It is 999 because it is as advanced, and different, in sales coaching as you can find. It is proven and very effective.

999 is new and applicable now (although many of the elements have not changed in centuries). 999 is not a process or a methodology, it is not training or a technique. It is coaching you in the differentiators, and how you can reform behaviours, and change your status from an achiever, to someone who is talked about with awe in your industry.

Some of the material contained is most applicable to complex solution selling, large capital investment sales or clients with whom you would like to enjoy more than one transaction. There are still many elements though, that if effectively deployed, will also assist the one time sales person enjoy increased sales. Remember, if you sell houses and you expect that many of your clients will only buy one in your area – if you handle the sale like a 999er, your buyers have neighbours, friends, colleagues, family, and conversations at bus stops and bars! Referral business is your key to repetitive success.

A Legend does not need to advertise!

If you read this book, and apply the key elements to your life and work habits, then you will significantly increase your success and your income.

I cannot guarantee you will be a legend, as I do not have a magic wand.

Only you can decide what to do with the information, observations and secrets that I share with you now.

These are the elements that have made me millions of dollars over the past years, and that I have observed in others whose sales strategies and exceptional ability to win consistently have made them respected legends in their industry.

I have disregarded the negative legends, they do not qualify as 999ers. These are the one horse cowboys and girls who rode in, took over any vulnerable town and then left a community in disarray with people shot and bleeding, and the stores pillaged.

The new millennium then arrived with its revised regulatory environments, industry and government scrutiny and a whole new code of ethics. These people found it impossible to practice their belligerent and arrogant ways and needed to clean up their strategy to survive. They were unable to keep their domino houses from tumbling and their troubled customers in hand. They too were legend, but for all the wrong reasons. Some of these people from the 80's, and early 90's boom times, took their money and ran – some stayed and burned when the economy and the environment changed.

Few survived. All are remembered by customers with varying degrees of negativity.

This guide is written in my own inimitable style - I write like I speak!

Editors tell me this is not appropriate for a book, much less a corporate book. However, I don't like reading text books and I know many of you don't either. I have already two books published, and my readers tell me they love the writing style because it's easy to follow, entertaining and they feel I am talking to them.

Either way, that is how I write . I hope you cannot just live with it, but can enjoy it too.

I tend to call it like it is. I am known for my frankness (my nephew tells me sometimes I border on being rude, but that's what he likes about me). To really explain to you the differentiation between a 999 Sales Legend and the average sales person, I need to be frank and open with you.

I have a weird Australian sense of humour, and I will try and manage it but I know that is going to come through here and there! So I guess I should apologise now if I offend anyone. Offence is never intended, I am a happy person who just loves people, so I have no will to offend anyone.

Many people who are high achievers suffer varying degrees of Attention Deficit, they lack the ability to sit still and be bored out of their brain by a book that is full of graphs and hypotheses, or the psychoanalyst theories of how we are, and why we do things.

I promise there is none of that in this book. There is no way I want to psycho-analyse any of the people I have observed, or even myself.

As 999ers, we are all very comfortable with who we are, we probably do not care too much what a psychoanalyst would make of us anyway, albeit understand most Sales Legends are a bit eccentric.

Now, before every psychometric tester, leaps all over me with indignation. Testing has its place, and if you decide to do 999 in a live coaching environment, you may well have to do a test before, so the coaches can see where you fit on the scale of loser to legend! They can identify ambitions and behaviours that may help or hinder you.

I will share with you a small personal story though – I am a bit of a story teller as I think it helps us grasp facts faster, with a more real life slant.

> *A few years ago a corporate psychologist told me that I was over optimistic, bordering on living in a euphoric state.*
>
> *I am still trying to figure out what the hell he thought was wrong with that, or was he just jealous?*
>
> *I am very happy with euphoria as a state of mind!*
>
> *He asked if I was taking pills. I actually thought that someone needed a reality adjustment if being happy was considered a problem, or only achievable through the use of stimulants.*

Ah, see your first taste of my humour. It is a true story though.

Interestingly, the psychometric test was scarily accurate about me, who I am and what I can do! They can be very helpful in establishing a start place, aptitude and progress.

Some of the things I will tell you I have observed or used, in solution selling, will seem ridiculously simple or obvious – but they are an essential part of the common denominator that identifies the 999 Sales Legend. Whilst they may be obvious to you and to me, they may not be obvious to someone else – it may be the key element they were searching for. The one that unlocks the door to greatness, but they missed it. So we will wade through everything together, even the fact that COO's notice your shoes!

These are the elements that make sales people millions of dollars every year, all over the world.

I will use as many true case studies as I can, I will change the names so I don't get sued by someone, but I make you a promise that everything in this book is true and factual. Every story and situation actually happened as documented.

Some people make millions and do not do everything in this book. I do not dispute that. However, depending on the element they choose to ignore – it may dictate how consistently they achieve greatness and for how long.

Many people do well for a few years and then crash and burn, sometimes to revive someplace else and do it again – some never to be seen again. This guide is about becoming a true and respected legend that understands, and is familiar with the art of replication. That is the ability to win, win and win again consistently exceeding quota, making club and having the income you want. All this without burning yourself into rehab!

Now we have all that explanation out of the way, let's take a quick look at the elements we will explore together in this guide to exceeding your own expectations.

999 Legendary Selling For The 21st Century is a holistic mentoring approach to understanding the elements of success in selling, particularly large solution selling. We will not only look at the selling elements, but also the image, state of mind and the personal integrity that sits behind the successful sales person.

First we are going to take a look at ourselves and find out if we are starting from a position, and reputation, of **Integrity.** Sales Legends maintain integrity with themselves, they know who they are and do not try to be anyone else. They truly understand what integrity means and manage any weaknesses to ensure they are viewed as a person of integrity.

Second, we will look at the very vital **Human Connection** in the selling role. Sales Legends respect everyone that contributes to their day, and their success. They make robust and meaningful connections with their clients at all levels and they have a large virtual support team in their own companies. They rarely use rank to achieve an outcome, because people want to help them. Everyone likes to be on a winning team, and that is what they create. They become trusted advisers at the most senior levels.

Next we will move onto **Political Reference.** Sales Legends do understand the environments in which they work and know the reality tree of influence and command. Their connections are spread wide and deep, they are not vulnerable to a reorganization. They can access anyone in their own, or their client, organization, at almost any time. They understand their decision makers personal needs – we all select a winning bid on two levels – personal and professional. The personal reason however can be much stronger than the professional one.

Hard Line Qualification is a critical success factor. Sales Legends know they will win because they only choose to bid for business they have fully qualified that they can win. Thus they will maximize their time and availability of resources to pursue opportunities that they know are theirs. Sales Legends will win an average of at least 8 out of every 10 bids they make. They will then go on to maximize further business within those clients, often excluding competitors from gaining a foothold.

Sales Legends have one outstanding quality that is found in every single one of them – the ability to truly **Focus** on their work when they are working. This extraordinary ability to focus allows them a better quality of life, and simultaneously increases their productivity and attention to detail in their sales.

Follow-Up is one of those elements that is so blindingly obvious, it is easy to forget to pay sufficient attention to it. More than half of the average day of a Sales Legend is spent following up a person, or aspect of their sales process. Checking that others, whose priority may not be *your* sales process, have done what they committed to do.

Now we are coming to a really interesting, but very critical differentiator, between most sales people and those who win, often seeming effortlessly, yet consistently. This is **Strategy**, the element where a sale that you could win, and should win, can be easily lost. Poor strategy is often the cause of a surprise loss of a large opportunity. Strategy should be developed for the client, but also for the individual bid or opportunity. A Sales Legend will be very aware of what strategy the key competitors are likely to adopt and be ready to prevent their perfect execution by proactively leading the sales process.

Some of you may have not had the need for **The Consortium.** Many of you will, with varying degrees of success. This is the most difficult bid, or sales, process. Many chefs in the kitchen, often without a nominated, or effective, leader and agreed code of practice. This is an exciting way to sell and win very large deals, however some very special skills need to be learnt to be consistently successful in this process.

I always get very passionate when it comes to generating **Customer Enthusiasm**. When your client is enthusiastic about you and your offering, then you have just increased not only your chances to win, but for referral business as well. Enthusiastic customers will go with you from employer to employer. They will always make time for you or open doors to other opportunities for you.

The Sales Legend is always working on personal and business networks to be truly connected. **Reputation and Networking** skills are a logical flow on from sound integrity, and will become natural to top sales people.

Finally, we are going to explore the ***Art of Replication***. How Sales Legends can win time and time again, how they can save time and money by being able to quickly adapt and apply existing work to another opportunity or client.

Once we have explored the elements that identify a Sales Legend, then we will look at how to maintain passion and energy long term.

To become a Sales Legend you will need to continue to excel as a sales athlete, year after year. There are pitfalls to avoid, and behaviours to celebrate and continue. Self motivation techniques and ways to maintain your mind, and body, at peak performance.

As I mentioned earlier, not all of you will become Sales Legends, but most of you can, and will, significantly increase your result relative to your input.

You will find yourself consistently able to replicate success, and thus create a holistic feeling of satisfaction, and happiness in your life.

Enjoy the road ahead, it is an exciting place for any sales person who is dedicated to their profession and proud of who they are!

INTEGRITY

Integrity

Integrity is defined as *honesty and soundness*.

It is essential that a Sales Legend maintains an honesty at all times about who they are, what they represent, and that they be honest in all dealings with a client and within their own employer. It is of course preferable that they be honest at all times, and in all things.

Never has it been more important than in the 21st Century, with all the regulatory change in recent years, to have integrity at all levels in your work as a sales person; to declare all conflicts of interest; and to be sure that what you are selling to your client will effectively meet their business needs. It is necessary to also be aware of regulations regarding discounting.

It is important to remember, that the smallest slip in integrity (the lie that didn't seem important at the time) can cost you everything in the end. Most importantly it can cost you your reputation.

First, we will look at personal integrity as this is the foundation of being a successful sales person. Yes, you can still sell if you are dishonest, but you will have to keep moving from client to client, from employer to employer; from region to region. A reputation damaged by dishonesty is almost impossible to repair, it is a long and hard road back to integrity.

You need to know and understand who you are, first and foremost. You must live in this person, and not try to be someone else. If you lie about your background, the school you went to, the place where you live or lived, who your parents were or are – then you are placing not only yourself at risk but also your opportunity to be a great salesperson.

Now, this does not mean that you turn every buyers' office into a confessional – that would not be a good idea! It does mean however, that you never lie about, or try to hide, who you really are. It does not mean that you live your whole life in your suit, or never have any fun. It just means that you must always remain honest with, and about, yourself.

> *Mike was a sales manager who worked with me a few years ago. Mike was a high achiever in sales, he was also a hunter and a fisherman in his spare time. He had a large client, where the key decision maker was a conservationist, and it was a concern to him that if ever his client were to find out he was a hunter he may no longer want to work with Mike. He asked for my advice.*
>
> *I suggested that he always park his natural 'hunting interest' outside when he visited this client. I counselled him against a 'confession' early in the relationship as it would have counted against him.*
>
> *I recommended that as much as possible he stay away from deep and meaningful conversations with this client. I suggested he hear his clients conservation view whenever the client wished to express it, and listen attentively without the need for ego and comment. Just let it pass, do not agree with something he did not believe, but also do not argue the reverse either.*
>
> *I advised Mike that if ever his client asked him about his sport, then he would have to admit as softly as possibly that*

he was a hunter but that he respected that it was an individual choice. He would need to explain that he was happy to hear his clients viewpoint, as it helped him make better choices when hunting. Try and turn the potential area of conflict into a positive.

We agreed that as Mike did not have a personal friendship with this client, normally professional decisions were made in best interests of the company. In the event that his buyer took offence, if it could not be managed, he would have to change accounts. If Mike remained in integrity, perhaps if it ever came up, then his client would take a professional approach – or even feel that maybe he could persuade Mike to hunt with environmental sensitivity.

The outcome was that it never came up, as Mike was not a personal friend and he always found enough common ground on which to connect with his client, there was never a need to discuss the matter.

Mike went on to win several deals in that client with a total value of around 10 million dollars.

Mike remained in integrity, and was ready to handle the objection to his personal sport, if it ever arose. The personal interest was not a professional conflict of interest, so disclosure was not necessary unless raised by the client as an issue.

The client was aware that Mike was a hunter, as the competitor had been sure to raise it as an ethical issue. The client told me, in confidence, adding that he thought about it but he considered Mike a very professional and trusted sales *person. As long as Mike never wanted to debate, or discuss it, with him he was happy to ignore it in the interests of a good professional relationship.*

This same type of scenario is common, where the beliefs, customs or interests of a key decision maker' are not the same as your own.

It can be handled professionally and within the boundaries of integrity. A good client relationship may still be enjoyed. However, be aware that there could be an instance where you would have to ask to be removed from an account rather than lose your company the business, this rational recognition of unresolvable conflict also forms part of the top sales executive.

Personal integrity must not be confused with a right to privacy, as we discussed earlier, you do not need to go and confess everything to your client upfront. However, you must be prepared to be open and honest if any subject is ever raised, or they ask you questions about it. If you already know there is a potential for conflict in a sensitive area, then do not under any circumstances get personally close to your client, keep a respectful professional distance whilst still generating as much warmth in the relationship as possible.

I was once in a situation in a foreign country, where at a dinner, a live animal was to be slaughtered at the dining table. I am an animal lover, and I could not go through this custom even with my largest client. I sensitively explained to my client that, whilst I respected their custom and tradition and I really did not mean to offend, that due to my own beliefs and customs I could not share this experience with them. I explained that I sincerely hoped that my personal cultural beliefs would not affect the professional relationship

> *we had enjoyed to date. It was a difficult and tense few minutes, but in the end I left with dignity and retained their respect, and yes I went onto to have an excellent professional relationship, and won the very large opportunity I was working on.*

From your personal integrity, will be formed a large part of your reputation, and that reputation often precedes you into a sales process. You may be called by a new client because you have an excellent reputation, and you will always be respected by clients for the same reason. Similarly, you are unlikely to be selected to work with a client who wants to skate on the outside of the regulatory controls, and this is a positive pre-qualifier for someone who wants to be a Sales Legend.

Apart from being in integrity with who you are, another factor in forming your integrity will be your image. It should match your integrity.

Look at yourself in a mirror, do you see looking back at you the makings of a true Sales Legend?

Or do you at least see a highly reputable and successful sales person?

To be in integrity, we must also have an image that fits the person we believe we are.

Our image reflects our self esteem, and our pride in our own life.

Image is not just about brand, or newness, or having the right pen, car or briefcase. Those personal tools should reflect you, with total confidence or else be entirely inoffensive.

Image is the presentation of the total sum of you.

There used to be saying in the IT industry – 'You never cause offence with a dark suit, a white shirt and a sombre tie!' Similarly, if you are not confident of reflecting your personality (or perhaps you are a super radical in your personal life) – then having a clean and sober attire, an anonymous leather briefcase, a solid pen (perhaps a company pen), and a clean and shiny reliable car are the basics that offend no one.

It is important that if you wish to reflect your personal image that you do this with attention to your own integrity, yet without alarming your client. Unless you are sure of your client, beware of skidding up to the front door in the latest Porsche, flashing, what may seem to your client, an embarrassingly expensive pen and reeking of brand name junky! Or arriving with heavy face jewellery in a conservative client, and the latest gothic suit from a designer at the edge! Your client may wonder if you are trying to prove something; or you are too expensive, or too radical.

You can drive your Porsche, but keep it low key. You may have a beautiful pen, but don't flash it, just use it normally and stay away from anything too brashly branded. If you are into gothic, you can wear black, but make it conservatively inoffensive for work. Very rarely does a Sales Legend wear face jewellery, except earrings for a female. Old fashioned, but prevents you offending anyone!

Again, we are saying that your image must be comfortable for you, it must make you feel good and very confident, and above all it must make you feel the level of sales person you want to be. It must also not offend your client. For example, if you are a female and you have a client with cultural beliefs that a woman should be modest, then a professional modest suit with a longer length skirt, will be the way not to cause offence. Whilst, male or female, you may wish to claim your rights to dress as you please – be realistic – it can cost you sales!

The same applies for a client you have not met, err on the side of conservancy until you know them and observe the dress code of those around them.

The most memorable fact to most clients is that everything you wear is clean, well presented and undamaged. Especially make sure your shoes are always cleaned and polished, you would be shocked how many senior decision makers notice this detail.

> *In a survey I conducted amongst C level decision makers about what they found important in sales people, more than half them mentioned clean shoes! They felt it reflected the attention for detail of the inner man or woman*

Ensure that everything you wear fits properly and does not embarrass your client, or you. Even if you are selling in the R rated industry, your client must never be embarrassed.

Little things can be surprisingly important.

> *For Example:*

> *Men - ensure your socks are appropriate to your image and are not showing serious 'wear' signs, and Disney socks are a poor choice if you wish to be taken seriously in the Big League. Ladies, always carry a spare pair of hosiery in your bag, a ladder or a hole is never acceptable for a sales person.*

Again you will be surprised that some top sales people overlook these details in their enthusiasm for the sale. Trust me – they do – and regularly! Some people will never notice, but to others it matters.

Ensure your business cards are kept clean and uncrumpled – use a case. Make sure you have business cards with you! Know the appropriate way to hand them to your client according to his or her customs.

Look in the mirror each day and ask yourself

'What would be my first impression of me?'

Your answer needs to be – 'a professional and successful sales person!' If not, figure out why not! Then take steps to amend your image until you are honestly satisfied with it.

You do not have to carry a leather briefcase, or wear a suit, to be successful. You just have to have an appropriate image for yourself and your industry, and the event you are attending whether that is a Board meeting, a factory visit or a social event. You may think this is old fashioned but it is not. It is just respectful, and paying tribute to your professional attitude.

Your image should be carried into your personal time as well, specifically outside the safety of your personal home and haven.

Remember, your client decision makers are also spouses, partners, parents, DIYers, and sports people. You may see them, or they may see you, anywhere at any time. You should still be in integrity with yourself. I can honestly say that I never see someone considered a Sales Legend looking like a train wreck in their social time. That same self esteem carries over into their personal life and image. Their clothes are appropriate for the occasion, and above all they are fitting, clean and in good repair.

Someone that I hold very much as a Legend, once told me, 'If you want to be respected in society, never wear a ball dress to ride your horse, and never wear your riding breeches to a ball' I think he was very wise!

Take that mirror now, and hold it up to your industry, and your clients. Look at your reputation, find out what people are saying about you and listen very carefully without getting upset if you hear something wrong or negative.

Perceptions are very real and very powerful. It does not matter if a persons' perception is right or wrong, it is for them the truth. If you think I am a pig, then in your mind I am a pig! You will tell others that I am a pig. Conversely, if you think I am an honest, professional sales person then in your world that is what I am.

If we discover misperceptions, then we need to take steps to change them. This rarely means me trying to convince you that I am not a pig, but actually demonstrating that I am not. This, hopefully, eventually causes you to review and change your original perception. Let us face it, the last thing I need, is someone going around telling other people that Terrie Anderson is a pig, if I want to be successful!

Now, you will never convince all of the people, all of the time. So, it is important to remain true to your integrity, be the person you want to be. Project that person into your daily life and thus minimise the 'nay sayers'.

I heard this story from a colleague recently. In hindsight it is rather amusing.

I was hired as the Sales Director of a large IT company, with a long way to go to get back on track. They had been missing sales targets rather badly.

After a client visit, I went to see the client service engineers to try and get some answers for our client who was experiencing problems.

After I left the area, having asked for maximum support and minimum resistance from the technical team to expedite a solution for the client – One colleague, who was primarily responsible for the delays, said to the others 'Wow, when she sat down, you could hear the clang when her balls hit the floor' Meaning – She is a hard woman.

The other colleagues in the technical area, apparently took exception to his interpretation, so they took it upon themselves to ensure my reputation was corrected before it was damaged by the utterings of a poor performer.

My reputation was of someone who could get things done, was fair with the team but believed in delighting customers and bringing in increased business. The other colleagues believed I had been consistent with my reputation, and respectful, but was someone who was only prepared to accept best effort from client support people.

One senior engineer told my detractor, "She treats everyone with respect, she never yells or makes unfair demands and let's face it, she is the one who may help us save this company.'

This is just one small example of how quickly a reputation can be damaged by a 'nay sayer', but it can also be repaired by others, if you continue to remain in integrity and treat everyone with respect.

If you want to be highly successful in a sales career, particularly in the big end of town, (i.e. selling complex solutions, or large value sales, to large organisations), then it is important to be able to manage any intolerance, impatience, or prejudices that you may have. It is preferably, especially when it comes to intolerance or prejudice, that you manage them so well, you manage them right out of your space!

Prejudice and intolerance have no place in selling. Period, full stop – absolutely no place at all.

As a salesperson, you must be able to sell to a client, regardless of the colour, race, religion, level of education, disability, rating on the 'pain in the arse' scale, or the incompatible personal interests of your client employees and decision makers.

To be able to remain in integrity, and do this well, it is best if you can rid yourself of such judgements. If you cannot change your heart, it will be tough to remain in integrity, but then you at least must change your behaviour and demonstrate genuine tolerance. You do not have to agree with anyone else' beliefs, to be tolerant of them.

I learnt a long time ago that we do not have to actually like our customers, they are not there to be our friends. We do have to respect them. Therefore, you do not have to share the same views as they do. You must however be tolerant of their circumstances; their race and religion; their culture, customs and background; their level of stupidity, brilliance or arrogance; and even be able to remain respectful when they are an out and out arsehole!

You do not need to step outside your integrity, and approve, or condone their behaviour. You do not need to agree with their activities, religion or culture. You just have to accept it is their right, and get on with the business of finding enough common ground to connect and close your sale.

You do have to be tolerant regarding most things, but especially sex, race, religion, and ability of your client. These are unchangeable factors, and if you have prejudice then you will never reach your own true potential, unless you can find a role where your only clients are those of whom you approve, or feel comfortable. That will severely limit your career path.

Now, I am asking you to be honest here. If you know that you do have a prejudice or, an intolerance, I am going to try and help you deal with it.

Let us say for example you have a problem dealing with foreigners, whether they be resident in your country, or just visitors who are part of an international decision tree in your client. This is what I would recommend you do:

Research all about the country, customs and culture of the people you interact with. Learn as much as you can about them. When appropriate, ask interested, positively framed questions about their culture. Most people appreciate your interest. Prejudice and intolerance are usually reduced, and often eliminated, with better understanding. Intolerance normally grows in us. It is born of outside influences that give us a poor experience, or poor expectation, of that which we become intolerant.

When we are born, we have no prejudice at all. We are open to learning, full of curiosity and accept all that does not threaten us, as normal. As we grow older we are influenced by the opinions of parents, elders, peer groups and sometimes we place ourselves in membership of 'exclusive' organisations, that in themselves, encourage intolerance. In essence intolerance is a learned habit.

A Sales Legend will not be affected by intolerance towards a Chinese buyer, an African descent buyer, a white Anglo-Saxon buyer, a gay buyer or a male, or female, buyer. They will not be affected by the religious choice of their buyers, because they will maintain always a professionally warm relationship, that is unaffected by personal choices.

I have managed to eliminate my intolerances down to one. I am still somewhat intolerant towards liars and dishonest people. When faced with a key decision maker with these traits, I place as much distance as possible, whilst maintaining the professional relationship necessary to close my sale.

Managing any intolerance within you, is a critical ingredient in becoming a highly successful sales person, living in his, or her, integrity with an excellent reputation.

Professional Integrity

Now let us take a look at Professional Integrity. This Century is a whole new world full of regulatory traps placed everywhere in organisations to catch an unwary sales person, or their buyer, and rob them of an excellent opportunity, or possibly ruin a career and even get you, or your client decision maker fired!

From when this guide is being written, in 2010, no professional sales person should engage any longer in inappropriate behaviour with any client, at any level, ever! If your employer asks you to do this, I recommend you consider your employment options.

Now I am going to be realistic here, for those of you negotiating across international boundaries.

What do you do if the culture of the nation, with whom you have to negotiate is a culture where activity considered inappropriate in your company or country, is commonplace?

Then I highly recommend that the only way you should work is via a reputable local channel partner. This way your professional integrity will remain intact, and your channel partner will take care of resolving any further issues that may, or may not, arise as appropriate in that country.

You should not knowingly take part in any 'extra negotiations' or even discussions. Nor, should you allow yourself to be made aware of any activity other than that required to make a genuine and legally compliant sale to your channel partner, mindful of all regulatory affairs that affect your company and country. I cannot stress highly enough the significance of this, to maintain your own professional integrity, and your career intact. This also removes unnecessary stress in your life. A Sales Legend will quickly die if you are imprisoned for illegal activity.

Do not inappropriately entertain your clients, or offer them gifts that are outside good business practice of the 21st millennium. No expensive gifts, or business dinners of goodwill, are any longer acceptable behaviour for a sales person prior to closing a sale.

Your competitors will very likely find out, and they will use it against you.

> *I was SVP of Worldwide Sales for an international IT company specialising in services. We were bidding for a very large opportunity inside a large multinational, fast moving consumer goods company.*
>
> *We were shortlisted down to two final candidates for the bid, one of these companies was a NADSAQ listed IT industry giant, with a reputation of arrogance. The company I worked for, also a public company, was smaller and known only to well established blue chip clients.*
>
> *It appeared briefly that the competitor had an upper hand.*
>
> *The client was known for a work hard, play hard culture. They liked to be entertained in every way, and lavishly. They covered for each other right up to the C level.*
>
> *We had a different strategy. I knew that the final decision maker was a man from a rough environment, with a hard won education and he played tough and rough. I also knew, from my research, that he aspired to a life of grace and elegance, so prestige and sophisticated company were important to him. He had enormous desire for a life where he would be considered a gentleman. So we chose to ensure that everything we did as a team reflected this aspiration of*

his, whilst our competitor played the old established hard ball game.

There were often requests, primarily to demonstrate his power, by the senior decision maker for meetings at short notice on the other side of the world. The competitor fell out of professional integrity offering often excessive entertainment of all variety to all members of the buying team.

We did not, we were acutely aware that our client was a large public company and we were a public company, so we did things a little differently. We arranged meetings in very sophisticated hotel board rooms with excellent quality working lunches and one fine bottle of wine - never enough to be considered inappropriate.

We remained in our integrity. We treated him as he desired to be treated, a man highly respected in his industry. Let's be honest, it was easy to stay in integrity– he was very powerful, and any person who could sign off a deal worth many millions had our utmost professional respect!

Our competitor gave us a golden bullet (you will learn more about these valuable tools later). They completed their final presentation in New York and knew that we were the last presentation before decision time on the winning bid.

They took the key decision maker for a memorable night out in the Big Apple, and as a consequence (that could be expected) he missed his plane to be at our final presentation on the West Coast. That was what they had hoped and *planned for. He had to call us and rearrange the timing. My team thought we had lost.*

To 'compensate' for their part in him missing his flight, our competitors offered him a seat in the corporate jet across the country. The competitor thought this would obligate the buyer to them. This was our golden bullet – if he accepted this privilege, I knew that he would not award them the bid! The regulatory stakes were too high. He did accept.

He came to our presentation, I was now in a position of strength and asked the closing question, and we won the bid. Our strategy of professional integrity had paid off very well, even to the point of causing a feeling of recklessness in our competitors sales team.

The result was that the competitor chose to complain to the Board Members after the bid was announced, that they had been taken advantage of. It was only a matter of weeks before the Board of this international company moved to dismiss several key decision makers, and the opportunity was resubmitted for bidding. However, we remained the only company from the first round that were invited to bid again with a new decision making team in place.

The lesson here is that the competitor who lost professional integrity never even got a chance to try again! To this day, that competitive company does not enjoy any market share inside this international consumer giant. Not only did the sales person not become a legend, but they took their company down with them.

Professional integrity means never accepting bribes, or gifts that are inappropriate. It also means never giving what your client may not receive. It is your responsibility to understand the regulations of your country, and the rules in both your clients' organisation and your own. It is your responsibility to play the game within those regulatory boundaries.

Do not offer your client excessive or inappropriate entertainment prior to winning the deal, nor promise a payment in kind (such as a lavish party) if you are awarded the business.

A Sales Legend of the 21st Century will never try to entrap his client, or compromise them in any way. He or She will know they have the knowledge, strategy, plan and integrity in place to win easily.

If you sell from a platform of both personal and professional integrity, then you will be in a position to build a fabulous sales career, operate with a greater sense of self esteem, and show your face everywhere, at anytime without fear of repercussions, or discovery.

"SALES LEGENDS ARE NOT BORN.

THEY ARE NOT MADE.

THEY DEVELOP FROM THE RESULTS AND ACTIONS OF PEOPLE WITH THE TALENT, WHO HAVE THE PASSION AND THE COMMITMENT TO LEARN.

THEY HAVE THE TENACITY TO APPLY WHAT THEY HAVE LEARNT, INTELLIGENTLY IN THE FIELD."

Human Connection

The Human Connection

This is the most significant differentiator between your average sales person and a Legend. This is the largest module in 999 Legendary Selling For The 21st Century. Some of this content you will already be very comfortable with, some of it may be a small revelation. It is a holistic subject, in that it cannot just be the way you are when selling, but will impact your whole life positively. This is about forming a habit of truly connecting with people on all levels.

Sales Legends demonstrate extraordinary ability to reach out and really connect with other people, particularly those people who can influence the result of their sales campaign.

Sales Legends operate at a level of communication far beyond the average person. They are not just communicating, they are actually forming relationships that last. Establishing bonds of commitment and support for their efforts. Team members in departments like legal, logistics, operations and engineering speak of these people with delight and hold them in the highest esteem.

Sales Legends can pull together the hottest, most proactive people into high performance virtual teams, that go on to produce exceptional results every time. These team members love working with the Sales Legends, even though they are usually demanded more of, and required to work harder, sometimes well out of normal hours. They love working in a winning team and the Sales Legends can easily share the recognition, without fear of losing any credit for themselves. This comes from the easy confidence that a Sales Legend develops as he, or she, wins great business consistently.

The ability to make high quality Human Connections is a very rare and powerful skill. I challenge that the reason it is a rare skill is because it is not taught in any sales courses that I have ever experienced. Believe me, I have experienced, sometimes suffered, many!

There are specific courses related to communication and conflict resolution, which I highly recommend as add-ons to further develop these essential skills. This subject is complex and requires a holistic approach to your communication habits, plus the ability to inject your passion, charisma and self into every encounter with another human.

> *Recently, a young person with ambitions and dreams to become a Sales Legend asked me what course he could study at Higher Education level that could assist him be a better sales person. He had noted that Sales was not offered anywhere in his country as a curriculum in higher education.*
>
> *I wish it was, I always have – if any recognised University would like to offer Sales as a tertiary curriculum, I would be delighted to assist them in developing material for a Commerce Degree majoring in Professional Selling.*
>
> *I was really struggling at first to offer appropriate advice, other than do some subjects from Dale Carnegie, and some other stand alone courses. Then I began to explore courses available and wonder what could be useful in selling – I decided that there were*

two subjects that may offer assistance in the higher education market.

My first choice would be Psychology. To understand this vital human connection. My second choice was Commercial Communications, although it had a lot of irrelevant content included. Both these subjects could guide a person to better understand the human element of a great sales person., You need to comprehend how to understand, connect with and motivate everyone around you easily without exhausting yourself.

The reality was though, that neither course offered the real understanding of motivation of self or others; neither course spent time really understanding how to make that amazing two way connection that results in lucrative, synergistic long term sales relationships.

The first ingredient needed to make substantial human connections is the core element of respect. As a top sales person, you must respect your client and their staff, you must respect the people whom you select to assist you to win the sale, and in general you should treat everyone with whom you have contact with respect. This is regardless of how they treat you!

It is a tough ask, but respecting people comes from a habit. Habits, good and bad, can only be formed over time and consistently doing something the same way. So here we see the requirement for a high achieving sales person to again take a holistic approach to develop a skill they learn into a lifelong habit. You will need to practice respect for everyone at all times. This is from a homeless person asking you for a spare dime, to the Head of your Country, Your client, President of your company or your parents.

Being respectful towards people does not mean condoning everything they do. It can be as simple as respecting their right to make their own choices and be their own person. It does mean always speaking with respect when we address someone, be that a stranger, our children, or our biggest client.

This type of repetitive behaviour can develop quickly into an unconscious habit of treating every person you meet with respect, even if you do not like them, or you think poorly of their behaviour.

You may be shocked at how often I witness lack of respect from good salespeople for those mortals they consider to be 'lesser'. I have been told 'they don't rank!' Yet sometimes, I have seen these people quietly sabotage the campaign of someone who treated them with contempt, they sure ranked then!!

It is not necessary for us to be rude, arrogant or to show people we do not like them. We can tell people we do not approve of their behaviour, but we must try and refrain from telling them we do not approve of them as a person. Disrespect is a fast track to increased stress in your life, and a lack of support for your initiatives like the next big sale process.

When you have a great human connection with others, you do not have to force people to work with you, support and help you, and you will never need to pull, or call, rank. Competent people will be knocking at your door, volunteering and asking how it is going – what they can do to help!

These same people in legal, logistics, engineering, finance (many of whom are known for their general dislike of sales people) will be talking about you. They will give you great reviews, they will warn you of traps and pitfalls ahead, they will really help carry you across the line.

> *I can recall instances of feeling slightly guilty because I could go home and enjoy a glass of champagne by the pool with my family, in the midst of a closing phase, whilst others are back at the office resolving contract or payment issues for me.*

> *They were doing this willingly, and cooperatively, because they understood I have done my bit, and they have the detailed knowledge, that I do not, to complete these tasks. They would tell me that I deserve the time at home, and I would be a pain in the butt if I were hanging about!*

That is the result of a great human connection with your virtual team.

Now we have established that the first skill to achieve such a level of human connection is respect for yourself and for others, let us move onto understanding the difference between communication and human connection.

Communication, I define as any contact, dialogue or even simplistic momentary connection. It can be one way – as in a lecture, or a message delivery. It may be shared without feeling or involvement. It is simply an exchange of dialogue, email, documents or a delivery of a message.

For example

> '*Would you like a cup of tea?*'
>
> '*Yes Please*'

Neither party to that communication may have even acknowledged each other. They may not have made eye contact. They are unlikely to even remember minor detail about each other. They may remember briefly a lack of respect, or that you were nice looking or that you had a certain kind of voice. It will just be almost anonymous. Yet this communication should be very personal, because they are offering you service. If you want a great cup of tea, make a connection instead of just communicating!

Human Connection is something quite special. It can be made for the simplest dialogue exchange, or it can be a meaningful two way enhanced communication. It can even be achieved in the delivery of a speech, it is possible to connect with an entire room full of people.

Connection touches the audience, be that one person or many, not physically, but awakening their inner being. It acknowledges their existence on the planet as a human being, and the service or message, delivered as something unique and private. They will remember this connection, and therefore remember you.

It is possible to connect with a room full of people, so powerfully, that your message and you, the messenger, will remain a brand on their subconscious mind for a long time. They will seek you out again, as the message felt like it was just for them and they made this rare connection with the speaker.

Over the years I have often been surprised by the power and

residue of connections I have made. It is both humbling, and rewarding, to hear back that someone with whom you connected with briefly, more than a decade earlier, speaks highly of you to others, remembers your name, recommends you and tells positive stories involving you that you do not even remember yourself.

If a human connection is made two-way, then a kind of magical event takes place. It is like a transcendental drug, you are both lifted to a high level of motivation and pleasure. Those connections will remain with you for life. Those people will care what happens to you and seek you out on Face Book years later to see what you are doing. They will in essence be the perpetrators of your Legend status, and accept subconscious responsibility for keeping it alive.

So now, let us start to look at how, beyond respect, we can make these powerful human connections.

The first impression is very important, if this is done well, then you never have to gain 'lost ground'. We have already resolved that your image needs to be right for you, and not offensive to your client, so now look at your approach. When you meet someone, move towards them calmly but project the warmth of respect for them, for their time given to you, and for the opportunity granted to make a new connection. They probably had a choice about what to do with this piece of time. You are the Sales Person, so it is your job to make them feel as comfortable, and happy, to be in your presence as is possible. If the air around your message is warmed, before serious dialogue commences, then connection is faster and easier.

As a top sales person, you need to exude confidence, charisma and warmth when you enter any situation.

Practice the effects of a great introduction in a mirror, with a trusted friend or on a recording device where you can hear the results. To sound and look genuine, you must be confident that you have a message to impart that will not waste their time. It is important that once you have the room warm, then you must quickly move to outline what it is, that you have come to do. You can do this in a soft, or a formal, way depending on your client and the relationship. Common ground is a great introduction to a subject.

For example:

'Joe Burgess, on your team, recommended that you would appreciate an outline of the new solution for the Security Division directly from us, so that you were in a stronger position to make an informed decision. We want to be sure that we uncover any concerns, or special needs you may have, and address those prior to the final bid........'

In this instance, Joe Burgess and the relevant solution are your common ground. If it is possible to tie it in even closer, then that is a plus.

For example:

'Joe Burgess, a fellow Rotarian on your team, referred me to you....'

or

'Joe Burgess, on your team, recommended that you would appreciate an outline of the new solution for the Security Division directly from us. Incidentally, I heard from Joe that you are a keen member of the Kensington Drama Club, this is an interest we share as my wife and I like to be involved with

our local school production each year. Not quite on your scale of achievement, but similarly very rewarding.

Pause – allow a response _ Then back to business with,

'Joe and I wanted to be sure that you were in a comfortable position to make an informed decision. We wanted to be sure we didn't miss anything, and to uncover any concerns, or special needs you may have, so we can address those prior to the final presentation'

These latter examples offer an additional piece of information that can form common ground. However, again you must be conversationally confident to use these factors, or it will sound somewhat false – or like you are 'trying'.

As a great sales person we must connect in those first few minutes, not try to connect. A bit later in this section, we will discuss the 30 Second Research technique that will enhance the first impression even further.

You are starting to deliver your message, the purpose of your visit and your audience of one, or many, has given you their attention and the room is warmed.

A great sales person never attends a meeting without a purpose!

What a waste of everyone's time. If you have nothing to contribute or no purpose, then avoid the meeting. Now is the time to capture the attention of your audience with great delivery of your purpose and message, ensuring that everyone is fully engaged and with you every step of the way.

Another rare skill, that is regularly found in Sales Legends, is the ability to actively listen. This means being 'in the moment'. Not thinking about your next appointment, or whether your car might be towed, or being flighty of mind. It means paying absolute attention to everything your client, be that internal or external client, is saying to you.

An important tip for the restless soul in many sales people:

> *The more boring it is, the more you have to pay attention, so that your mind stays in the moment.*

It is when your client feels that you are truly listening they will appreciate your time very much. Show you are listening, by acknowledging sentences; by asking intelligent questions; by making notes, if necessary, to stay on track. Do not allow yourself to wander in your mind and engage in humorous mental asides such as wondering if that is a wig he, or she, is wearing!

Stay in the moment. This is something you can practice in social situations with family, friends and new people you meet. As a value add, you will begin to see an amazing new quality to your personal relationships, especially family, if you can learn to do this well.

In fact, go try this now. Go and engage a family member in a conversation. Practise being absolutely in the moment and actively listen to them. Try asking your child about their school day, that will be good practice. If you get monosyllabic answers, (then you probably reside with teenager!) try to draw them out beyond their yes and no, that is a response designed to block you out. Practice your open ended question techniques.

Dealing with a child like this, can be almost identical to the skills you need to deal with a difficult client!

> *Recently I was at our Club. It was noisy around the bar as lots of people were engaging in some form of communication.*
>
> *A good friend leant across to me, and commented ' So many people talking, and no one listening!'*
>
> *I looked around, and objectively observed for awhile, and he was absolutely right.*
>
> *Listening is an art that is indeed rare, but highly valued.*

It is possible to listen to someone, saying little for a long time, then hear back that the same person told someone else you were an interesting and intelligent person. Why? They do not even notice they are doing all the talking!

If you practise some observation for the next few days, everywhere you go, you will see people talking but their audience is not listening.

I now understand that if someone is not listening to me, then I have failed to make the connection. It is my fault.

This is a situation best avoided by someone wanting to become a Sales Legend. It is not so difficult for great sales people to connect using the coaching in this guide. Make conversation when you are prepared to put the effort into the human connection, or you will blend into the blah!

Understanding Modes of Communication

To make a strong verbal connection we must understand as much as possible about our audience. i.e. the other person, or people, we want to connect with

Those of you that have had exposure to NLP (Neuro Linguistic Programming) will be able to grasp the significance of quickly assessing what primary modality your audience uses to communicate. NLP has its controversial side as a therapy, but it does simply explain a method most of us use to communicate.

By being able to recognise and, even better, actually communicate in, the primary modality that your audience uses, it can strengthen the impact of your message dramatically.

It is much easier when we know our audience well, such as family members, friends, work colleagues with whom we interact on a daily basis etc.

However, we also need to learn how to do some *30 Second Research* when we meet someone for the first time. If we really want to connect with them, and have our message understood. This is a great tool to use.

Once practised, it becomes automatic and happens at a sub-conscious level.

In the first 30 seconds that you meet someone, observe as much as you can about them, and their surroundings. Let us quickly overview the operational senses, and from this, you will begin to understand what to look for in that first vital 30 Seconds.

This will prove very useful knowledge for you, if you want to enjoy success and repeat business.

Overview of The Operational Senses

Each person we meet has a mode in which they operate dominantly. There are three main senses we use to interact:

Visual Sense (Seeing)

Auditory Sense (Listening)

Kinaesthetic Sense (Feelings)

Most people use all three modes, in a variety of mixes per person, however each of us is usually dominant in one of the senses.

> *For example the colleague sitting next to me is probably around 50% visual, 30% auditory and 20% kinaesthetic. This means when I communicate with him, I use as many visual words as possible, draw pictures of what I mean both literally and figuratively, and talk things through usually repeating the message to reinforce it. I use less 'feeling' words. This way he hears my message, and sees my meaning quite clearly.*
>
> *This is not so difficult, because I am also very visual.*
>
> *However another colleague on my team is probably about 70% kinaesthetic, 20% visual and 10% auditory. This is kind of the opposite end, of the communication scale, from me.*
>
> *So I have to express everything a little differently when I*

> *speak to him.*
>
> *He does not 'hear' my message easily, and he does not 'see' my meaning, he needs to 'feel' my meaning. This is difficult, because I am lower on the kinaesthetic scale, so I have to use a mode of communication in which I am weak. Some other team members get into conflict, or shut down, with this young man because they do not understand how to connect with him.*

On every team, and in every family unit, and with every group of friends or colleagues there will be a lot of misunderstanding just because of this simple miscommunication technique, where we do not hear, see or feel the true integrity of a message delivered.

Often this misunderstanding remains a silent attention killer, so no one is aware that one person, or even a few people, got a completely different idea from what was said.

Sometimes two people can be arguing about the same thing, but neither can express their ideas in a way that is comprehensible to the other. This is due to the different communication modalities. This is a shame of course, as ill feelings and frustration can arise when there is no need, they are actually in agreement. They just do not recognise it.

30 Seconds of High Value

When we meet someone, we need to listen very carefully to how they express themselves in the first few words. Listen for things they say that represents feelings, visual or auditory signals thus giving indicators of their primary modality.

Do they say things like 'I feel' or 'I see'?

Where are they looking when they talk to you?

A visual person will have locked onto your eyes and face.

An auditory person will be focussed on listening and not watching. They may be flicking their eyes around your facial perimeter, the ceiling, and the walls – they may notice what is happening around you, but still be very aware of what you said.

A kinaesthetic person will be looking usually down, at the floor, the table, or a fixed space nearby your head – but rarely makes eye contact for more than a second or so.

When you shake hands, a visual person will probably make eye contact immediately.

An auditory person is likely to spend some seconds ensuring the hands connect, and then make shorter eye contact.

A kinaesthetic person may try and avoid your eyes altogether.

The handshake itself should not be considered for this purpose, the type of handshake may be affected by cultural background, customs, health or confidence.

If you have the chance to be in the physical space of the person, then look around.

Ask yourself:

What can you see to give you information for your quick research?

Is the space filled with interesting things? Visual people usually need things to look at to occupy their mind.

Is it filled with family photos? Kinaesthetic people like to have familiar warmth nearby.

Is it lacking a personal touch, or filled with gadgets?

For example; auditory people like phones, recording devices, speakers, music, and are less likely to notice bare walls.

None of this is foolproof, but my research over about 30 years, has demonstrated it is a fast, and reasonably accurate way to establish how best to connect with someone.

Now that you understand a little more about how to do your 30 second research, we need to explore how to use that information to effectively to make a good connection.

If you determine that your audience is visual, then you need to communicate with them in 'visual' terms. This can be difficult if you are, for example, strongly kinaesthetic, but with practice you can. This is because your natural way of communicating, in this example, would be kinaesthetic.

As I mentioned earlier, I am very strongly visual, almost an extreme case, yet I have taught myself to communicate in all three modes.

Now, I do not say that I am perfect at this, but every time my communication screws up, I know I missed the chance, because I did not take the time to communicate in the mode of my audience.

Once you have this knowledge, it is to your advantage to make use of it for effective communication. It is never the other party's responsibility; remember it is you that wishes to convey a message, and sell something.

I have witnessed some amazing conversations between two people who both understand this concept, and they each speak in the language of their audience. This way both people are maximising their understanding of the other, and truly making a memorable connection.

We will look at ways to connect with each modality, however remember some people have a very even modality balance (e.g. 40% -30% -30%) so they will have powerful influences of all three. In this case you need to use all three and we revisit this at the end of this section.

If you determine the primary modality of your audience is:

Kinaesthetic

With a kinaesthetic audience you need to limit eye contact, particularly for prolonged periods of time. Whilst we are often taught that eye contact shows honesty, and that is true, many 'feeling' people find it confrontational.

Some of the best scammers can look you right in the eye, as they remove your watch from your wrist! They will be visual people!

Try sharing the same eye 'prop' that your audience uses.

For Example:

> *In business meetings this is often the table or desk With kids, it is usually their shoes, your stomach or the table; and with someone at the bar - the bar and the glass will feature as eye props.*

Express yourself in a feeling way. This audience needs to 'feel 'the meaning, as they have less focus on hearing and comprehending it, and may not be able to see it, or you making grand gestures, in front of their eyes.

If you are selling to a 'feelings' person, then you need to make them understand how they will feel when they buy your product.

For example, if you were selling them a car, you would need to communicate something like '

> *'Imagine how you will feel driving down the freeway with the wind in your hair, your favourite song on the radio and your family beside you. You will feel so proud of your new car.'*

I will use this same car example again for each of the modalities, so we can make understanding this concept as simple as possible.

If you want to hold a conversation with a kinaesthetic person, then again express your thoughts in a way that helps this person 'feel' their effect, because they are less likely to 'get the picture'

If you are in their environment, observe, then at an appropriate moment ask about their family (the ones in the photos), or how they 'feel' about a relevant industry event, or a news event. You could ask them about their hobbies and their life, and then extend that conversation into areas in which they will feel comfortable.

Focus on how they feel about any subject.

As we discussed earlier, one of the most important communication techniques, is the art of listening. Part of a great listening technique is learning to ask appropriate questions that encourage your audience to participate further in your conversation, willingly and happily sharing information, because you have made a good connection.

Remember with an audience strongly embedded in 'feeling' be sure to phrase even questions into the feeling mode.'

> *'How do you feel about?'*
>
> *'What does this mean to you?'*
>
> *'Do you feel you will move towards?' etc*

This type of audience will appreciate genuine warmth from you, and a feeling that you understand where they are in life.

They will not appreciate fast, brash techniques, and are often more easily offended by, unfiltered or misunderstood, words than a visual person.

If you determine the primary modality of your audience is:

Auditory

This person hears every word you say, and usually likes to talk.

When I meet a very auditory person, the first thing I notice is that they are often like a waterfall. The words keep spilling, but sometimes can be characteristically uncoloured, even completely disconnected to the rest of their body. Visual people will use their hands, and speak in colour with lots of adjectives to describe their picture, but auditory people are unlikely to do this.

Some auditory people can talk, nonstop - whilst driving, running, shopping, working, cutting up the vegetables for dinner (if I did that, I would have no fingers) and they can even talk when anyone else is talking! They do not necessarily even notice.

Sometimes, they can talk quite dispassionately, not seeming to take time to consider the feelings, they just need to describe the event in words.

Some auditory people are listeners only, they rarely speak more than a few brisk and practical words, but they hear every sound, every undertone. Their opinions about you and what you are selling are formed predominantly by what you say.

If you have a sense of humour like mine, it can be easy to accidentally cause offence. My humour is more visual and abstract and I do not necessarily mean what I say – the deeper meaning is expressed on my face or with other visual signals. An auditory person may miss these additional, but important signals.

Unfortunately, if you, as the speaker, are not careful with your words, your auditory audience may 'hear' something you said, a slant or angle, that was not intended. It is a misinterpretation, as they may not be balancing the other modalities, of the speaker, with the words.

If I ever offend someone, it is usually on a telephone call. Because my auditory sense is somewhat low, I do not hear what I say in the same way an auditory person may hear it. Therefore offence may be taken when not intended, or even considered! This is not the fault of anyone, but it is my responsibility as I have the knowledge and should have recognised the difference in modality, and have made a better connection.

Most auditory people will have strong influences from 'feelings' and/or 'visual' so they will not be so extreme. You will be able to mix a couple of modalities in your communication but try to keep auditory dominant.

The auditory audience needs you to explain, in words, very clearly exactly what your message is. This is the method that radio advertisements have to use; as obviously they are only reaching your auditory sense.

Your sentences will need to be descriptive, but without necessarily painting a traditional picture.

As you are being well heard, it is a good idea to throw in a few visual and feeling references, as they will hear them and then use their second modality to add to their understanding.

Use words like:

'I hear what you say'

'I understand what you are saying'

'This is an interesting story to listen to'

'I cannot believe I am hearing this'

'I can hear some concern in your voice'.

Your questions can be framed with examples such as:

> *'Can you tell me what you heard about?'*
>
> *'Did you hear the item on the news about ...?'*
>
> *'What did the kids/manager/neighbour tell you happened?'*
>
> *'Did you hear that we launched a new product that might suit you?'*

If you are selling them that car, you would need to rephrase your statement to

> *'Imagine driving down the freeway, listening to your favourite music with the family telling you how happy they are in the new car – by the way did you hear that motor? Sounds really safe/hot/cool (as appropriate)'*

Your genuine warmth can be expressed here in a way that they can actually hear it in your words.

Use warm words, use expressive words. This is a chance to enjoy your language in an artful and interesting way, because this person will really hear you!

If you determine the primary modality of your audience is:

Visual

When your audience is dominantly visual, then you need to paint pictures with your words. This person sees their world, and what they cannot physically see, then they imagine in a picture. If you describe your new house to them, they will visualise it in their head immediately.

They will usually talk about seeing things your way, or their way.

Their language will usually be full of adjectives, and descriptions that include colour, shape, style and the order of everything. This is because they speak from the picture in their minds.

If you ask them about their holiday, they will tell you what they saw.

If you are not visual, then try to imagine describing a photo, and that will help you communicate with a visual person. Visual people are the greatest story tellers, because they talk in pictures.

In their space, visual people are usually surrounded by visual distractions, and reminders, such as art, postcards, photos of places, holidays, events (often including family), ornamental objects, kids art, souvenirs like a bottle top from a fun party and a screen saver on their PC.

These people usually love colour and visual drama or 'eye candy.'

Often lighting, (too much or too little), will affect their mood and maybe even their health and wellbeing.

To reach a visual person, use language like:

> *'I see'*
>
> *'I want to show you'*
>
> *'Let us see if we can cover that later in the presentation'*
>
> *'Let me demonstrate'*

> *'What do you see as your main problem?'*
>
> *'What do you see as the ideal solution?'*
>
> *'Where do you see this going?'*
>
> *'Can you describe what you have in your mind?'*
>
> *'What is your vision for...?'*

To sell them that car you would have to rephrase your statement to something like;

> *'Imagine owning this car in gloss red with white leather, driving down the motorway and watching the mountains slide majestically by. The family looking great beside you, watching your GPS guiding you with ease and the look of envy from your friends when they see this hot red machine glistening in the sun'*

You just sold me a new red car ☺

Your genuine warmth needs to be seen. Your facial expression and body language are more critical than ever, as this audience is watching.

You need to have a genuine smile, and you need to show you care.

Ensure good hospitality with this kind of person if you want to impress them, because the more the surroundings match their taste, the happier and more comfortable they will be.

You want them to relax and give you their attention.

Mixing The Senses

Now, as I said earlier most people are a mix of modalities, so as much as you can you need to balance your communication and tailor it to suit your audience.

Let us take a look at what should happen when you cannot establish a clear dominant modality, or you have a larger audience than one key person.

Now you will need to present everything, as much as possible, in all three modalities, so you do not alienate anyone. This is tricky to get right, without appearing to repeat yourself, but it is very possible.

The most outstanding public figures, the ones that really appeal to the masses, can do this very well.

In their media interviews, they repeat their key message three times. Each time in a different abstract way, so the listeners do not notice. Why? Because each listener remembers the message in their primary modality, and mentally does not recognise the repeats, or screens them out!

Listen to some radio or TV interviews of elected presidents, or leaders of excellence in large corporations and you will see this technique demonstrated, you can learn by listening and through practice.

> *John Chambers, President of Cisco Inc, is a fabulous example of connecting with every person in the room where he speaks. One of the best Corporate speakers you can observe in action. Watch the total connection and absorption of his*

> *audiences, even when his message is kind of the same as his last keynote!*
>
> *John Kehoe is a Master of the Law of Attraction and a fantastically engaging communicator. He connects with every single person, his communication feels personal to you.*
>
> *Barrack Obama, President of the United States of America, engages his audiences in all three forms of the senses. He does it with consummate ease, and you never notice the repetition of a key message.*

Repeating yourself, does not work quite so well in a smaller social situation, like Friday evening drinks, or even in a small meeting. On these occasions you can use a modified technique.

Each time you talk about a subject, in a social or more private situation, you can change your modality regularly.

You use all three methods of communicating – visual, auditory and feeling.

A sentence like 'I *heard* about the accident in the High Street, I *saw* on the news that the driver had been drinking, imagine how the store owner whose window was broken must *feel*;'

Not so difficult is it? But we rarely practice it. This will really connect you to the group you are with, on a personal level.

This technique can also work well if we are unsure of the modality of our primary audience, we can express ourselves in a way that we know he, or she, will retain the message we want to deliver.

Alternatively, you can focus on a couple of key decision makers and deliver the bulk of your message in the primary two modalities of the most important audience member, with reference to asides for the other members in the third sense.

Remember that respect for everyone we speak to, and genuine warmth towards humanity helps everyone hear, see, feel and understand our message, and our intent.

How well you can communicate at this level, will be how you are remembered, and talked about, by other people in your community, your work, and your public life. We become the messages we represent.

How well you connect, on a personal level, will determine the quality of your relationships with clients, family, friends and impact your career. The comments of your colleagues, their respect and feeling of being connected to you, will determine your future in any industry.

In a world where everyone is talking and no one is listening, we need to effectively deploy tools such as these.

We must really reach out and connect with our audiences to become a Legend.

Your conversations will be worthwhile, your messages will be remembered. It will be less frustrating, and more fruitful. You will easily make acquaintances, you will be remembered as someone who listens and cares, and you will be more successful as a result

Strong communication is a direct precursor to success.

A Sales Legend is a great communicator who connects at every level.

The Human Connection can be at all levels, and everywhere you go.

This leads us to the first 999Legends Success Secret, it was given to me by a respected Master, as The Philosophy of One Minute More!

One Minute More – *Legends Secret Number One*

This is one of those secrets I promised you at the beginning of the book.

This is a secret that will make you truly memorable to thousands of people, everywhere and every day, you will add to your list of connections. Using this secret will have an immeasurable payback, and it is very significant in fast tracking your legendary sales success.

> *I first met this Master of Human Connection when working as GM in the regional office of a large global services provider. I hired Kamal as a senior sales executive. He was born in India, but had lived in New Zealand for many years.*
>
> *Kamal told me he knew, personally, more than two thousand people in New Zealand, and they would recognise him. To be honest, I did not really believe him but I did believe he was at least well connected.*
>
> *After a short time of working with him, I realised he was probably conservative in his estimate of how many people knew him. If you were to walk to the cafe with him to buy*

lunch, it was an amazing experience. People from all works of life, would smile at us and say 'Hi Kamal'. On one day I observed that almost everyone, from a street cleaner to a senior Government Minister, had acknowledged his presence in just a few hundred metres.

My regional VP was planning a visit from another country, and he had asked that some important meetings be set up for him. This man was not so useful at the client face, as he was a little arrogant, and often too technically detailed. My team felt he could actually damage a sale process at senior level.

I was a little concerned about how to meet his requirement and yet protect our opportunities. Kamal asked what I wanted to arrange, and in a moment of fantasy I commented I would rather he met the Minister for Telecommunications than a customer.

Kamal walked over to his phone, and was able to call the Ministers' private secretary and connect immediately. He was able to arrange the meeting on the spot for a few days hence. Normally an impossible feat, as you had to write weeks in advance, with justification for an appointment.

Jokingly, and slightly in awe, I commented that if I had known it was that damned easy, I would have asked for the Prime Minister instead!

Kamal quietly said, 'if you would like our VP to meet Jim (the then PM of New Zealand) I can arrange that', I knew he could!

That week I sat Kamal down in a meeting room with a coffee, and asked him to explain his secret because it was like magic.

You must remember his title was 'Senior Sales Executive' and he lived in a normal home, in a normal suburb. He drove a company car. He didn't show off, or have huge wealth or historical family connections. He was actually a gentleman living a simple and normal life, yet he could connect in an instant with some of the most powerful people in the country.

He gave me the gift of a powerful secret:

'The Philosophy of One Minute More'

and I am now going to share that secret with you.....

One Minute More is what you give every single person you meet, or interact with. It begins with a smile and an acknowledgement of that person, not just their job function. It involves making eye contact and actually seeing them, and realising they are a person just like you or me. They have a family, a history, a story, a life away from their work – just like you and I do. They may work the same hours that you or I do, and be paid much more or much less. They contribute in the same way we do. Then, when we have transacted our business, we give them one minute more . We make a human connection.

These people are your lunch provider, your cleaner, a manager, a bank clerk, and airline check in person, a supermarket check-out person, a man or woman with no home and living on the street, a fellow driver at the gas station – the list is endless.

At best, most of us maybe nod and acknowledge them. At worst many of us just ignore them, and expect them to process their task without recognition. Some of us even shout at them when we are not happy.

However, the miracles start to take place when we accord them one minute more. We truly acknowledge them as another human being. They become aware that we know they have thoughts and feelings, and that we appreciate what they do for us, or even that they exist.

This is not so hard as it sounds, I have concluded that we interact with no more than between 10 and 30 people a day. So at an average of one minute each, that is not a big task or investment. The returns however are extraordinary.

As Kamal explained to me, each person has relatives and friends. Their uncle or brother may be someone of influence, they may clean the home of the Minister, they may be an extraordinary athlete, the possibilities are endless. We do not know the story of every person we meet. Also each person has their own power, and that may be exercised on you – for better or for worse!

How?

Well, the lunch provider determines what quality of ham and salad sandwich you receive. They have the power to enhance the enjoyment of your lunch with the freshest ingredients in abundance, or not. The cleaner can win, or lose, you a big deal by their attention to detail. The person who serves tea to your clients can actually influence how they feel about the company. It is obvious what people in more senior or powerful positions can do.

In Kamals' case, his route to the Ministers private secretaries was originally via the valet in his garage. He was a law student, with a part time job and the nephew of one of the senior ministers! He knew all of them personally, had played with their children.

You will never know each day how any person you connect with is connected in the world, or even if they will help you or provide a tastier lunch or a better airline seat. However, what you will find is that the goodwill you generate will take care of most days for you, and eventually you will be so well connected that you can arrange miracles like Kamal.

This One Minute More just requires you to acknowledge each person, smile at them, ask them about their life, their day. You can comment on something they are wearing, or a new hair style, or tell them you appreciate how well they do their job. You can empathise for an earlier rude customer you observed. It can be as simple, as actually making eye contact with your waiter and thanking him for the drink he just delivered. Not mumbling thanks whilst engaged with someone, or something else. Or worse, ignoring them altogether because the person you are with is more important.

This is such a simple thing to do, yet it is complex to explain to you. It is something you must use every day and then you will begin to enjoy the accumulated benefit of it.

> *My partner and I, enjoy many rewards from giving One Minute More.*
>
> *We are frequently upgraded in hotels and airlines, we mostly receive wonderful service wherever we go, people remember*

> *us and are delighted to see us walk into their restaurant or business again.*
>
> *We also experience miracles of connection on a regular basis, and have even received new business directly as a result of making what seemed an innocuous and simple connection.*
>
> *On the rare occasions, when we receive poor service, we use One Minute More to change the situation, it usually works very well.*

I recently had a question from one of my coaching students about why would he want to connect with a street person. I told him that it was because he never knew what would happen, that one day that person might save his life, or tell him he had forgotten to take his cash from the ATM when distracted. (That actually happened to me).

Additionally, I explained to him, it was about habit and not being superficial. Once you have acquired the habit you do not consider what you may gain, you just know that energy will return itself to you one way or another!

The Law of Attraction – *Legends Secret Number Two*

This now brings us to a discussion about the Law of Attraction and Abundance. There is a lot of noise around at the moment about the book and the movie 'The Secret' which explores The Law of Attraction.

I suspect, many of you are now emotionally and mentally pulling back.

Possibly you are thinking 'This is New Age crap isn't it?'

Maybe you are thinking, 'I am an engineer, a pragmatist, how can I even contemplate this rubbish!'

Or maybe you have an open mind, or even further still you already use these laws every day to assist and support you.

Regardless of what you think today about The Law of Attraction there are a lot of your colleagues out there deploying the principle daily to their benefit – and maybe to your detriment. Better to understand it, and decide for yourself whether it has merit you would like to deploy. It has become a familiar and very valuable friend that I use daily in my life and work. It isn't even so difficult to understand if you have a basic knowledge of quantum physics.

My suggestion is bear with me, understand the principles and then make an informed and intelligent decision about what you want to do with it.

It is not a religion, although some would possibly present it that way. I have attended groups where it was spoken of with great reverence and like a 'cure all', the healer of many. It is not a cure all, nor a law that allows abuse by the dreamers, or the lazy folk.

It is not a cult, or knowing people who speak in strange tongue to each other. It is simply an observed law of the flow of positive, or negative, energy by many successful people. It requires you to take positive, confident action and intentionally direct your energy.

Understanding this principle will assist you in other elements of becoming a Sales Legend like focus, commitment, human connection, strategy and the art of replication. It is well documented in a myriad of ways from the ethereal to the downright practical application.

The Law of Attraction, is just like any other scientific law.

It is what it is. Do what you will with it.

It will not change, it will carry on about its business regardless of you, or what you think of it.

It is not new, below is a famous quotation that encompasses use of the Law of Attraction. It is one of my favourite and is beside my screen. It is read, and referred to frequently by our team. It was written by Goethe in the late 18th Century.

Goethe was someone from whom Darwin drew inspiration and knowledge, when writing The Origin of Species.

Both men are Legends in their own fields.

> UNTIL ONE IS COMMITTED, THERE IS THE CHANCE TO DRAWBACK, ALWAYS INEFFECTIVENESS.
>
> CONCERNING ALL ACTS OF INITIATIVE (AND CREATION) THERE IS ONE ELEMENTARY TRUTH, THE IGNORANCE OF WHICH KILLS COUNTLESS IDEAS AND SPLENDID PLANS
>
> THE MOMENT ONE COMMITS ONESELF, THEN PROVIDENCE MOVES TOO
>
> ALL SORTS OF THINGS OCCUR TO HELP ONE, THAT WOULDN'T HAVE OTHERWISE OCCURRED, A WHOLE STREAM OF EVENTS ISSUE FROM THE DECISION, RAISING IN ONES' FAVOUR ALL MANNER OF UNFORESEEN INCIDENTS, MEETINGS AND MATERIAL ASSISTANCE WHICH NO MAN COULD HAVE DREAMED WOULD COME HIS WAY.
>
> BOLDNESS HAS GENIUS, MAGIC AND POWER IN IT.
>
> -GOETHE

The third and fourth paragraphs refer directly to the Law of Attraction.

Assuming we can accept that every human generates an energy field, then The Law of Attraction is simply a law that explains how that energy flows and interacts with the energy of other humans, and other life forms right out to the planetary and Universal order of things.

Everything we do has a consequence, a domino ripple effect, and we are totally responsibility for our own actions; Therefore, if we can learn to project our generation of energy, to assist us in the creation of what we desire, we will be in a stronger position.

Why doesn't everyone use this, if it is so simple?.

I challenge you it is so simple that people refuse to accept the existence of it. It is also so simple that people stop using it. It is easier to slide back into the morass of human tragedy, than to learn a new law and rise above it. Even to the level that no one will likely show sympathy for you anymore, and some enjoy receiving sympathy. You would have more control over your own results, especially accepting total and sole responsibility for our actions. Not everyone wants that level of responsibility, not everyone can be a Sales Legend either.

Have you ever wondered why some people always park their car right where they need to be? Perhaps you are walking 500 metres in the rain from your car space. Some people get the good tables at the restaurant, but no matter how early you book you are always at the back?

The Law of Attraction works quite simply.

Once we commit to a goal, in this case a very simple one (parking the car) the energy we generate in making this commitment is expended from us, so it moves outward. Much in the same manner as the expanding Universe, and the unfolding leaf.

Our subconscious mind is very connected to the energy that runs everything in the Universe. It is exceedingly powerful, it can bring things to you that you confidently request and plan for.

Always remember everything has a price, and we must be prepared to pay the price for what we want (not necessarily a cash price).

Whether you choose to believe it or not - that energy, that we commit to parking the car, goes out and causes a whole series of events to happen that would seem unimaginable. They do occur, and we attract to us the very thing we seek.

In this case, a car space where we want it.

Sounds ridiculous?

Just try it a few times and see how it works!

We never park our car on the next planet, we always park our car where we expected to, in a convenient place.

Just Lucky?

Every time?

What are the odds of that being luck?

Try this simple example, and decide for yourself, how useful that would be if you could use it for grander plans!

> Next time you leave home to go somewhere, mentally visualise and book your parking space right where you want it. Trust that it is there for you, and drive up and park. Occasionally, I have had to go once around the block then it was there, but never more than few minutes delay and usually none at all.

I want to share with you a simple story.

> A few years ago, I was having coffee with a senior sales executive friend of mine who is usually quite a stressed person. Sally and I shared our Christmas Shopping experience.
>
> I mentioned how easy it was this year. I had gone to a particular shopping mall, I parked my car near the door where I always park it – I went in and found the gifts I needed – I took them to the gift wrap bar – I went to the lovely Oyster Bar for a glass of champagne and rock oysters, seated at a nice table – I collected all my beautifully wrapped gifts – left the mall and drove home. It was a lovely day.
>
> Sally said ' Well you were lucky. I went to a shopping mall but I chose the worst day. I had to drive around 40 minutes to find a car park, and then I was 400m from the mall. I could only find two gifts, then the gift wrap bar was too busy, the Oyster Bar was fully booked and I could not get a table, so I drove home very frustrated'. I had a lousy day but then that's typical for me at Christmas'

Imagine my surprise, when I discovered we were in the same mall, on the same day.

We had arrived just ten minutes apart.

Why the difference?

Well, I expected what I received – a nice, relaxed day enjoying the pleasure of selecting nice gifts for my friends and family. A nice light lunch, and a glass of bubbles.

She expected a huge hassle because it was Christmas time and everything would be stressed.

We each got what we had expected and planned for!

That is again a very simple account of the Law of Attraction actually working. The world is in balance, think of yin and yang, and the age old wisdom behind it.

Many people project negative energy and attract poor results, why should that be you? There is an equal opportunity, the mirror image, to attract positive results!

We get what we plan for, what we book, what we pay for – it does not discriminate between rich and poor, good and bad, it just delivers what we expect. Trust me if you live with an expectation of receiving crap, you will get crap regularly – you spent time attracting crap!

In a Sales situation, the same law works very effectively. To win consistently, you must know you can and will win. Then you can apply the same law you use for parking your car to a greater cause and greater reward. As our energy is not a limited resource, we can still use it to park the car ☺

We cover this idea of knowing if you can and will win further under the Chapter of Hard Line Qualification.

> Applying the Law of Attraction, you will receive pretty much exactly what you expect and plan for. If you are not confident in your ability to manage and create the result, then you will have varying and often unexpected results.
>
> Why does this work?
>
> Well, in a sales situation, we should only experience doubt if we have planned insufficiently, if we are unprepared for what our competitors are likely to do. Our subconscious knows, and remembers, the short cuts and risks we took and whether we deserve to win.
>
> If we have appropriately done our planning and strategy, we know our client and they know us, we understand our own weakness and strength in the sale, we are in integrity with ourselves, we respect our teams and we understand our competitors behaviour then we deserve to win! Or we will be warned that we will not win ahead of time, and should not be wasting time.
>
> Ensure your subconscious is giving you the right message, because you have done all you need to do.
>
> Sales Legends experience very few surprises!
>
> If we have confidence, we can commit to winning. If we commit to winning, as Goethe advises, all manner of unforseen assistance will flow our way.
>
>> *I was a Regional Director for an International Security Company. We had a sales shortfall in our month. We had*

only 6 days to go, and we had written only 25% of our target, this had never happened before. This month we were besieged with client side delays in major projects we had expected to close.

Most of you will understand and feel the pressure we were under. We needed for that month 680,000 usd to meet target. We had always exceeded our targets, everyone was feeling down. I decided to apply a visualisation of the Law of Attraction.

First I told every member of the team from the cleaner to the management team, I knew we would make the number. I believed in them as a team.

Then we taped an A4 page with just 680 typed clearly on every booth, in the bathroom, the kitchen and the meeting rooms. We told any visitor who asked that it was our number for the month.

There was not a person on staff who had any number but 680 in their minds. Our technical support team said initially it was no good them having 680 on their desk because they didn't affect sales – yet on day 5 our largest sale for the month came via a technical support guy who saw a client with an opportunity where we could solve a problem. I do not believe he would have recognised the significance of that opportunity had he not been aware of 680.

The consequence was that on day 6, at month closure, we had billed 681 of solid, yet mostly unforseen business.

This guide is building your skills in a collective way that you can take and move forward with. Let us briefly summarise what we know right now:

From today onwards, try to retain and use this very simple secret of applying The Law of Attraction and the Secret of One Minute More.

Plan for greatness and success, plan a winning campaign. If you plan for less, you will get less.

Then take action towards your goals and plans, always be honest with yourself and others. Give a fair deal for a fair price. Expect to receive the same and do not settle for less, and do not ask for more than a fair deal.

Radiate warmth and empathy towards people, listen to them when they speak to you, stay calm and in control. Plan, plan, plan and follow yourself up. Do always what you believe is right. The rest of the elements in this coaching guide will strengthen your arsenal of skills even further. Keep it handy as a reference along your path to greater success.

Making Commitments

No more secrets in this chapter, but instead some sound practices that distinguish a Sales Legend from the bunch. You should be sure you understand these, and choose to exemplify them.

There is one very simple practice that all senior clients, I have ever interviewed, comment on:

'*The best sales people are those who do everything they say they will do.*'

How simple is that?

Yet, simple as it sounds, apparently very few of us actually do it!

I find that so amazing, but it is true.

If you tell your client, or a member of your support team,' I will call you on Monday' – Damned well call them on Monday!

Even if it is to say that you do not yet have the answer. Call them when you said you would, every time, never miss it.

You will find it hard to imagine how much your client, and your virtual team, will appreciate this very simple, yet vital act of commitment and follow up.

Now, I apologise to you if you are one of the apparently single digit percentage sales people who actually do this 100% of the time. I have met many very good sales people, most of whom only do this some of the time.

This is such a simple practice, yet so neglected and so obviously frustrating for buyers. Ensure this practice is also adhered to by all members of your team by following them up. Eventually, they will know that you care if they honour commitments, or not.

Your client may actually be quite excited about your solution, and be looking forward to Monday, and then you let them down. Perhaps they have a broken piece of office equipment, and you have a shiny new machine that they really want – then on Monday they are eager for your call, and delivery of their solution to a problem, then it doesn't come as promised. Instead of an enthusiastic customer, you now have a disappointed customer.

Instead of having a great human connection, you have a broken connection.

Many clients will now call a competitor, when maybe you never even had one!

Your team will likely only ever be as attentive as you are. If you let them down, then you let yourself down.

Perhaps your legal adviser set aside an hour on Monday to work on your contract, but you failed to call them back with a critical piece of information. They may feel disappointment, and a sense that maybe this contract is not so important after all. You must act with the same sense of reliability, commitment, urgency and dedication as you expect from your support team.

Next is another simple, and probably glaringly obvious, practice that cannot be overlooked.

Always deliver value in your sales process.

Delivering Value

If you can only sell on price, if you have a reputation for dumping the price at the end of the quarter, you have trained your customers to react appropriately to get the best deal.

> *Running a region for a service provider, I used to regularly use this technique to improve my profitability on large deals. The hardware and software for my clients were all third party products around which we added value services. The profit on many of these product lines was unacceptably low.*
>
> *It was possible to predict by supplier what sort of additional discount I could gain at quarter end for a large order. The vendor sales people had trained me, the decision maker, very well.*

On the last days of a quarter, I would improve my profitability (quarter on quarter) by an average of 20%. There was no added value, there was just price!

This is a form of reverse selling, in these deals, the decision maker was calling the shots and had a strategy well executed. Remember, I had nothing to lose as the client – only gain.

There was however, one supplier where this never occurred. Respect for the sales person called Jane was high, there was an excellent human connection and they had become a supportive and trusted adviser to our business. So much value was added in the sales process, that the extra discount was irrelevant and unnecessary.

Jane did not sell to me based on the best price, instead my team were supported all throughout the sales cycle. She was responsive to our needs and supported us in the end customer. Jane was always finding ways to add value to our pitch for the business, and as a trusted extension to my sales force, assisted us to close sales consistently.

A sales person with low margins and high market share, unless specifically required to gain market share at any cost, either has a defective product, or a poor ability to understand the generation of value to the client. They are not, and never will be a Legend.

Sales people who regularly practise win/lose as a strategy will never be a Legend, in fact they will be fast forgotten.

Admittedly, some clients only buy on price. In this instance it would form part of the strategy for that sole client. However many sales people, that I meet , use price as the main reason, or excuse for gaining, or losing business. Many of these are high achievers, but at what cost to the company, and for how long before they need a new company in which to plug their umbilical cord right beside their unintelligent sales processes. Actually, anybody can sell on price alone. They will win probably half of their sales, but with high stress levels and eventually 'gunslinger' reputations. They can be easily replaced, a Sales Legend cannot.

A Sales Legend knows if they lost a deal, that they were outsold and it was their total responsibility.

If you work for a true value added supplier, who does not wish to sell on price alone, then this should be part of the Hard Line Qualification process, and we will explore that later. If the decision will be price alone, and you work for a profit oriented solutions provider, then you should not be bidding in that deal.

Value comes from attentiveness through the sales process, including all the elements you learnt in sales 101 plus the mentoring from this guide.

Value comes from how you structure the proposal. Perhaps you can find a way to add more value, and make it hard for the client to compare apples with apples, as they say.

Value comes from truly working closely with the customers' team, understanding their business environment, and what business problems they need to solve with your solution. Value is in providing them with an ideal solution at a cost effective price. Most clients seek value for money more than just price, but it is a misconception of the lower level, or lazy sales person, that it is price alone.

In short, value comes from a service level.

Value never comes from price alone, in most cases your price just has to be justifiable.

Relevance of Time and Messaging

You are busy. Your Client is busy. Your Teams are busy.

You are the only one with Focus on your Sales process, all the others have multi focus. They have their own jobs, possibly multiple sales contracts in negotiation, and it is unlikely that your sale will be the sole focus of their life.

A Sales Legend only takes time from an internal, or external, client when they have a relevant action to carry out. They do not disturb people to just 'chew the fat!' or to be seen.

If you request a client meeting, you must have a relevant message and a purpose for that meeting.

It can be discovery of information needed to finalise your proposal. It can be to present relevant information, it can be to check on progress, but it may not be because you think it is time to have a meeting. Nor can it be because your competitor had a meeting yesterday.

Every time you ask your clients for time, there must be a reason that you can clearly articulate up front, and that justifies them giving you that time.

If you are introducing your manager to a client, ensure your manager is well briefed, and that he or she has a subject of relevance to discuss. If not, delay the meeting until you do.

I have experienced a senior manager who wanted to justify his existence by meeting clients, but rarely with a purpose. He was however socially quite a pleasant man. He became threatening when I tried to block him from client meetings. My team refused to accommodate him, and I preferred not to stress them.

I solved it by asking a few clients that I knew really well to spare him a half hour, but clearly setting the expectation that this was a PR exercise.

I could usually compensate my client by arranging the meeting over coffee, light lunch or a beer after work. The discussion would primarily be about common ground, or interests, and occasionally one of my client s would cheekily ask him for a discount for an existing service. (Now that made my manager want to run).

This way the client at least got a personal benefit, a pleasant half hour refreshment break. Expectations were set and met.

It was better than letting this loose cannon in with an important client about to make a buying decision!

When you ask your client for a meeting, ensure you explain simply why the meeting is required. Be open and honest, but if you are trying to gain competitive intelligence then you better have an alternate good reason for the meeting. It better be a viable reason, or your alternative agenda will become blatantly obvious and appear somewhat underhand.

It is never appropriate to ask your client for competitive intelligence. It is however possible to enquire if you may know who your competitors are, although you must be gracious if your client refuses to divulge this. It is possible, although skating close to some regulatory ground, so be aware – to ask what your client likes about your competitors product or service. However be prepared you may open a Pandora's ` box, as they may also share this information with all competitors. Some companies have a policy like this.

Whatever your message is, and whatever the reason is that you are asking for time, make sure it is relevant and that you respect the time allotted strictly. If you are granted 30 mins, plan your visit to deliver your message in that 30 minutes, still considering all the other elements such as respect, warming the room, finding common ground etc. If you ask to meet your buyers' manager, you better have a great reason for such a request. It is a normal and common request, but ensure your contact understands and can articulate to his manager why he should make the time to meet you.

If you need to approach the C level, which in all large solution sales is usually highly recommended, then be very, very sure you have relevant messaging to that level. Trust me they do not want to hear about the bells and whistles of your number one technology!

Always have your 30 second pitch ready in case you meet an important business influencer in a social situation. Despite what you learnt in Sales 101 or 201 - Never pitch it in the elevator unless invited to do so, it could cost you everything!

If you meet a very senior person in any informal situation, it is fine to introduce yourself and explain why you are interested in his, or her, company. Unless invited to do so, do not then continue into a ten minute pitch on the spot, it may well be extremely inappropriate.

Better to try and take One Minute More and make a great connection. You may then be invited to explain your solution at an appropriate time, and you will be remembered well.

Never be late, and if due to complete disaster you are – phone 5-10 minutes ahead of the appointed time and try and reschedule the appointment as appropriate in their diary. Some of you may be annoyed that I would mention such a basic, but again you would be surprised how many sales people with many years experience do not afford this simple courtesy.

Excuses that are unacceptable in most client sales appointments include, but are not limited to:

- A Flat tyre
- A traffic jam shorter than half an hour unless caused by a major accident that will be on the news!
- Weather, unless entirely unexpected and severe
- A late train or bus
- Someone else fault
- An overrun in a previous appointment

Why? Because each of those events should have been foreseen, and your planning should allow that you arrive early, with time available to change a tyre.

This is all about planning when wanting to be a Sales Legend.

Consider this Quote from a COO:

> "I have had sales people arrive 10 minutes late for a half hour appointment because 'the traffic was bad on the motorway'. That traffic is bad on most days at that time, what sort of idiot do they think I am?
>
> I know they didn't leave any earlier than they would at a different time. I even know they will use that excuse again and again.
>
> If a sales person let another meeting overrun, that is not my problem. That is their time management problem, they set meetings too close or failed to set expectations of attendees that they need to leave on time."

I do not know many senior managers who feel any differently. We want to meet with people who respect our time and who want our business enough to plan and respect their meeting times.

> I have even had a sales person who arrived 30 minutes late, become angry with my assistant, because I could no longer see him.
>
> I had another appointment. He did not seem to understand why his problem should not be my problem, and of course my next appointments problem!
>
> He regaled, to my assistant, his struggle through adversity to reach my office! His adversity was simply a block on a motorway exit, that to my knowledge was always there at that time of the day.

> *His frustration and anger with my assistant cost him any chance of increased business with our company.*
>
> *If that sounds wrong to you, get a grip, it is reality in many situations.*

Your Customers Business Environment

They should have taught you in Sales 101 that understanding the business and industry of your customer is essential in winning trust and respect. Not least of which, it is also needed to construct intelligent offers.

There is an added element here for a Sales Legend. If you want to win consistently, then you should also understand who already wins regular business in this company, and why. They may not be competitors, but suppliers none the less.

Why do they win consistently? What is their strategy? How do they handle the hierarchical structure? Are there influencers you did not know about, or even suspect?

This can prevent you from having to invent the wheel and save many hours of investigative time.

> *Sam, a colleague of mine does this incredibly well.*
>
> *He calls it the friendly short cut. He selects a non-competitive company that does very well in a potential client. He seeks out the relevant sales person and actually sits down with them and talks through the types of strategy used, the political map and the basis for decision making in that company. He sets up a supportive coaching partnership*

where they can go to each other for support or advice, or even introductions when appropriate.

The information he seeks is safe, and not confidential. He seeks answers for what sort of sales strategy they use, what things that sales person considers is important to his client, such as high levels of service, or a particular dislike of sales people who park in the customer car space!

He asks how to get an appointment and connect with a particular executive that he has trouble contacting.

This can never be done with a competitor, but provided all regulatory issues are considered, then this can be an interesting synergistic approach to having an additional understanding of your client.

It is in your interest as a top performing sales person, to understand every possible element about your customer, their business needs, their political framework particularly as relevant to a decision process, and their pet likes and dislikes.

Maintain a Professional Relationship

Most of you will already be very aware of this need to maintain professional distance, but for the few who maybe have missed it in their previous training, I am obliged to include it here. Remember, this could be one of the small elements that have prevented you from becoming the Legend you deserve!

It is very important to ensure that at all times, no matter how much common ground you share with your customer, no matter how much you actually like each other, you must maintain a professional relationship. This does not mean you cannot share regular golf or tennis games, it does not mean you cannot spend social time together. It does mean that at all times you must place the business relationship first, and your behaviour must reflect this level of professional relationship and never compromise you , your company or your client.

A Sales Legend always remembers that this is a client and maintains a professional distance, no matter what. A warm and close bond can be formed but they would never consider their customer a personal friend, never!

Of course, never form a sexual relationship with a client. This is dangerous, possibly leaving all parties open to regulatory issues and embarrassment. If you meet your soul mate in a customer, then one of you needs to change roles or possibly even employers! As a sales person with responsibility for closing a large deal, you will need to advise your manager of the situation as soon as possible.

Another trap to avoid at all times is forming a secondary business relationship with your client. i.e. Something like your client invests money in your part time internet business, or your Wifes' cafe. Just don't go there!

This crossing from any form of professional relationship, to a personal one, nearly always ends in grief – or being denied the business.

You can do business with friends, but it is a difficult and precarious path if it involves substantial amounts of money in a sale process. You must declare your potential conflict of interest in most situations. Your competitor is likely the perpetrator of the situation becoming an issue, it could form part of a potential strategy to discredit you, or prevent you from bidding or winning.

Corporate Governance

We have referred to the regulatory controls surrounding, especially public companies and public entities, several times already under integrity and professional conduct. However, as ongoing regulatory change has created a relatively recent series of traps for sales people, it needs a little further exploration.

There are many sales people out there, who are still operating under the conditions of the 80's and early 90's. Often, it is because you have been coached by a manager from that era. Usually one who has not fully understood the implications of the new corporate order, or perhaps chooses to ignore it. Sometimes, because you find yourself in a high pressure sales environment, at quarter end, and you are asked to (or ordered to) step outside certain boundaries to close the deal.

Every person with a desire to become a Sales Legend, or even a high achiever in demand by employers, should take the time to understand the compliance requirements of their own company and any organisation with whom they partner, or sell to.

Now, I understand many of you have not the attention span required to study the regulations – I agree, it is hard going! So, have someone else do it for you.

Go to your legal department and ask them for an 'overview', they will most likely be delighted that any sales person has taken this time to ensure their own job is made easier. We sales folk are often the stuff legal nightmares are made of!

You could also ask an analyst or researcher to do this for you, in the event there is no legal department. If you are unfortunate enough to have no fiscal support, then you will have to do this task yourself, or pay someone to brief you.

> *I have even gone as far as getting a briefing from the clients legal department, that way I am very sure what my boundaries are.*

> *Very few sales people do this, and potential Legends know how effective this is for enhancing their reputation, whilst protecting their arses at the same time!*

Corporate Governance is not only a restrictive boundary it also opens opportunity to do things differently from your competitors, and gain advantage. I have found that generally by understanding my boundaries, I can be even more creative with strategy.

> *One sale that contributed to my own personal Legend is still, apparently, firmly entrenched in the minds of some people. I was even told just last week that this story is used in a legal class as a lesson in using corporate governance for advantage.*

> *I was working with my team on a significant three year government contract for the supply of equipment to all their several thousand offices. I had a very strong competitor who was tipped by the industry to win, in fact several vendors did not even want to bid on that premise.*

> *However, I knew we had several competitive advantages.*

> - *Our equipment was already installed and running successfully in the test environment, plus Head Office.*

- *The Decision Maker had a strong professional relationship with several members of our team, particularly the technical consultants and the front line salesperson.*

- *Familiarity with our system, plus plug and play functionality, meant a minimised roll out time and training requirements.*

Our competitor also had advantages that were strong:

- *Price, they could offer a better price to gain market share. Price was highly weighted in government decision criteria*

- *They were a more substantial company with better annual results*

- *They had more features in their boxes*

- *They were a highly aggressive sales organisation with a very legendary leader.*

One differentiator was we were nimbler of foot and quite humble. They were somewhat arrogant by reputation.

The key decision maker, at the client, had indicated a concern that we may lose on price, when the final bids came in, and that could mean the department would have to make wholesale change in their equipment and waste existing investment. They wanted to avoid this, and also they wanted to maintain our technical support team.

Time for a great strategy, but nothing obvious was a solution.

In my overview briefing of the regulatory environment, I found my strategy. The regulations required they must arrange at least three competitive open bids by tender, however the regulations did not specify that they could not choose a technology first. So for the loss of a small amount of margin, we opened this bid to channel partners rather than bidding directly as a vendor.

This meant that when the Request for Proposal was released it stated simply, in the first line:

'We require offers for the supply of hardware based on XYZ technology'

We had won, as a vendor, before the bid was even released.

Several channel partners bid, and our competitive vendors could not bid at all! We had eliminated them by taking time to fully comprehend the applicable Corporate Governance in building our strategy.

The key competitor went ballistic, and went to the highest levels of government to try and have this contract stopped; however each time the lawyers reviewed the case they advised that everyone involved was compliant.

It was a real win, win, win. The channel partners who got a chance to bid were ecstatic to be included, so we won more support from them. Due to increased competition in the bid, the customer received an excellent price: value ratio and had the technology they wanted. Apart from winning the deal, we were suddenly projected into the spotlight as a company that was going places, thus our enquiries for solutions increased.

It was even huge fun!

As a consequence, I was also aggressively headhunted!

So, if you previously thought the regulatory environment we must operate in today was a tad boring, remember a Sales Legend would open their minds to the potential gain from being on the front foot with corporate governance.

Arrogance

I had a lengthy debate with myself, and others, whether this short section should be in Integrity or Human Connection, because it belongs in both. However, arrogance does not necessarily adversely affect integrity, in fact it may even been born of a sense of righteousness. Arrogance does however have a huge impact on the Human Connection – and it's all bad news!

If I hear loud and clear one thing from decision makers, it is that they really hate sales people with an arrogant attitude. They also hate companies that behave arrogantly. Now, a company is not a living entity, it is the sum of its people – if a company is perceived to have an arrogant stance, then that will be a projection of the arrogance of management and sales people primarily. Those are the main client contact people at the senior levels.

To be confident, highly professional, yet humble, is indeed a common trait I find in Sales Legends who consistently prove their shiny star position at the top of the sales tree.

Let us establish some definition to ensure we are on the same page:

> **Humble**: *not considering yourself, or your ideas, to be more important than other people's*
>
> **Arrogant**: *behaving in a certain way because you think you are more important than other people:*

So we are talking about a very simple concept here.

Even if you are the best salesperson you know, working for (in your opinion) the premier company in your industry, you are no more important than anyone else. Everyone who does their job extremely well is in fact completely equal. Those who do their job not quite so well, are not necessarily deserving of a contemptuous attitude either.

Let me set some ego battering facts right before your eyes.

> *The cleaner does not clean the toilets properly, and in the middle of your final presentation, your key decision maker needs to use the facility. He, or She, may return in a very unsatisfactory, and distracted, state of mind. I have been in a team where the main subject of discussion after an excellent presentation was not the solution presented, or the messenger, it was the unclean state of the bathrooms.*
>
> *The Caterer does not have a professional approach to hygiene and your client team depart with a healthy case of salmonella all round. They are unlikely to have a sense of humour about this.*
>
> *The Receptionist is having a bad day, and is rude to the CEO*

> *of your client company, making him wait whilst she finishes a personal phone call.*
>
> *You are presenting to a large banking client. The engineering team accidentally put the wrong diagram in your presentation, and it is the diagram of another banks' confidential network.*

What I am demonstrating very simply here, is that every one of these people, even some who you may have considered less important, can bring you down.

Therefore, humbly accepting that you are no more important than any other member of your team will help you project a warmer image, and make a better human connection to the team.

Similarly, accepting you are no better than your clients' team will also help you make an enhanced connection to your client, and as a consequence you will be better informed. Not least of which, you will not be part of that league of arrogant sales people that most clients detest.

You should also consider that your competitors are also filled with great people doing potentially an equal, or even better job trying to outsell you. To be arrogant towards a competitor is very dumb, it just ups the ante.

> *I was in the closing stages of a very large Greenfield opportunity to supply all the Communications Installation and subsequent services to a new airport. The contract was valued at many millions over 10 years, and it was a complex solution with tight time frames.*

Just prior to the final presentation, I attended an industry luncheon and was privileged to be seated at the Head Table. Next to me, was seated the Sales Director of a very large Telecommunications company, and he was my key competitor in this airport bid. What a coincidence!

I had not met him before but had checked his name tag which identified him when he sat down. This is common practice for me, in case the person next to me represents an opportunity for a new client. I love networking.

I introduced myself by name only, and mentioned I had heard he was a finalist in the airport deal. This was definitely a time to be humble!

He smiled and said that "Yes, it was down to only two companies now.' He went on to arrogantly volunteer "Actually, we have already won. The other company is a small setup with only 50 people on the ground, they could never measure up to us, don't even know why they bother. The airport just uses them to justify our selection."

Now, I am a bit of a specialist in using a sales persons' arrogance against them. I congratulated him on his win, and went on to enjoy a fine lunch and keynote, truly excited by our prospects now. Our competitor did not even rate us, how good was that? They were unlikely pulling out all stops to win.

I was the GM of the local office of a very large international company, so although small by comparison locally, we had extraordinary experience in the transport industry, specifically airlines. I knew we could win, and he had just handed me, unknowingly, my golden bullet.

Naturally, for the final presentation to the airport board of management, my team were in fine form, especially as they accepted this feedback as a challenge to their integrity. Some had even bought new suits for the day, as we really cared about winning. We were the final presentation, a preferred position to have.

In my closing remarks, I told the Board "I want to tell you, that winning your business is very important to us. We are not a huge organisation here in this country, but we are certainly big enough to do this project, very well funded and supported by leading experts around the world in airport design who are only a flight away when we need them. In very large organisations sometimes a project, even of this size, is so run of the mill to them that it is not treated with the reverence it deserves. I can assure this Board that this will be one of the most important projects in our local history, and has the attention and support of our management worldwide. I promise we can do a great job, and you will be on time and on budget with us"

It was my golden bullet, and using the arrogance of my competitor against him, I had just shot them in the heart!

The Airport Board wanted to be the most important contract on any suppliers list. They had a time sensitive mission critical project to deliver within budget and on time. The eyes of Civil Aviation globally were on a new International Airport!

The simple truth of my statement, motivated by the arrogance, of my competitor was very powerful.

We won!

If you know you have an arrogant competitor, this is a legendary weakness that you must take advantage of. The peculiar thing about an arrogant competitor, is that they rarely recognise why they lost, so this tactic can be used against them repeatedly, with little energy and planning on your side.

A little humility means you feel unafraid to ask questions to ensure you have clarity of your clients needs. Better to feel a little stupid, than lose a deal! It means you are approachable, so that your client feels at ease and can ask you a seemingly stupid question if they wish. It means you can use information like a laser, effective and cuts to the edge.

Arrogance has no place in selling. Confidence is essential, and some ego is normal – we just have to check ourselves that ego does not manifest itself masquerading as arrogance!

Making sustainable human connections starts from the first impression and then grows warmly into a supportive professional relationship that can last a whole career. People are complex, relationships are even more complex, so if you reach out and make great human connections you are already fast tracking to peak performance

"THE MORE BORING IT IS, THE MORE YOU HAVE TO PAY ATTENTION, SO THAT YOUR MIND STAYS IN THE MOMENT."

POLITICAL REFERENCE

The Political Reference

In previous sales training events, you will have visited this subject in varying degrees. We are going to take a thorough look at how this should work.

I have noticed that whilst many people understand this subject, and the importance of it, very few sales people actually have this element fully under control.

I regularly see, even senior, sales people who know the importance of political coverage yet will often only have themselves covered vertically.

> *Joel was an excellent sales person, he regularly achieved his quota. He was working on a very large opportunity and he knew that he should be able to win it, so he really focussed on closing this in time for his quarter end.*
>
> *Joel understood political mapping in his clients, and he had a map drawn up for this opportunity in Acme. He then made sure that he covered off the key decision makers for this particular opportunity, which was a critical infrastructure project, for Acme.*
>
> *See over the page for his political map. He had covered everyone marked on his map in bold. It was reasonable coverage, except that it did not cover the business units affected by the new solution, and he had been told that the VP of Engineering was not a key person in this decision.*
>
> *What happened to Joel was a common tragic error in political coverage. The VP of Operations, the primary decision maker,*

suddenly resigned. The interim VP of Operations was the VP of Engineering, and as the project was critical, a decision was still made before a new VP was appointed.

The Decision team was now the CEO, VP of Engineering and VP of Sales whose new CRM was the catalyst (and funding) for the new project. Joel lost the deal to another supplier, and only achieved 30% of his quarter as a result.

He made a classic error. His political map needed to be wider, so if a domino fell in a line of command, he would still be covered.

Joel's Political Map for Acme.

CEO	
Chief Strategist	
CFO	
COO	
VP Sales	
VP Operations	**Director Infrastructure**
VP Engineering	**Technical Evaluation Team**
VP Marketing	

The first important step in any Sales persons understanding of political reference, should be a thorough understanding of the politics of their own organisation. Now we can all choose to be above the politics, and so we should, to achieve what we want. However, if you are not fully cognisant of the politics in your own company, you will likely fall foul of it.

That will cost you opportunity and support. That sounds ridiculous when you are a high achieving sales person, but it is reality. You should not play in the political arena, you should not have time. You should however, be very aware of how to make it work for you and your client. Also, frankly speaking it does not help your cause; or you ability to make great human connections if you piss someone off, whose support you may need, with a major political mistake.

So, number one if you can't quickly and clearly articulate who in your company is a decision maker, an influencer and who is considered a loser, then you better get onto it right away. Additionally you should know who are the wolves, and who are the hyenas.

> **Wolf** – *Moves stealthily and quietly throughout the entire organisation, knows their way around and who is doing what; who is capable who is not; can cut through bureaucracy to get things done; has respected and easy access to all including the CEO and even Board members. Never contributing gossip but often observing and listening. Asks a lot of questions, and actively listens to answers. The wolf does not name drop or call rank, they do not need to. They are often given urgent projects to lead.*
>
> **Hyena** – *Also prowls quietly around the organisation, but*

usually with the purpose of identifying a winning opportunity to be seen to be part of. Hunting without the effort of the actual kill. They form fast and short lived connections to groups until the objective is achieved, then move on quickly to the next opportunity. Takes credit for the ideas of others and is on the closing stage of every successful 'team' although no one noticed them there before! Often sends out thank you emails for a project they had minimal, or no, involvement in.

They virally spread information, and misinformation. Usually they have lot to say. Although people are often confused what the hell they are talking about, it sounds great. Bonhomie and humour form part of the Hyenas repertoire.

They are even known to schedule conference calls and meetings that they do not personally attend, due to other supposedly 'important' events in their sphere.

They seem untouchable, magically connected to the power names they keep dropping.

A Sales Legend would manage the Hyena, and befriend the Wolf, obtaining only benefit from both relationships.

Try to be also aware who is stable and who is not. The last thing you want to do, is parade before an important customer a colleague who departs the next week for your biggest competitor! It can still happen of course, but the better your finger is on the political pulse the less likely you will be surprised.

Go as far as drawing up a political map of your own company and mark it up the same way as you would a client map. Keep it safely at home, this is not something you need to share. In the wrong hands it could be misinterpreted.

Ask colleagues about people, listen to what they have to say to help you place each person in the correct place on your map. This will also help you match people when tier selling in your client.

Tier selling such as VP to VP, Director to Director, VP to Director with some common ground is a very powerful way of replicating influence. Your tier selling techniques will be improved by knowing something about the important people in your organisation, as it will assist you make synergistic matches to your client map. We will discuss how to make most effective use of tier selling in a later element – Customer Enthusiasm.

Now that you understand your own organisation properly, it is time to layout a competent political map for your client. This will form a part of your strategy as you will then clearly understand who you need to reach, with what message, and how to get them to hear your messaging effectively.

You need to take a similar approach in your client. First establish who is your mentor, and supporter, inside the client organisation.

If you cannot identify one, then either you are very early in the sales process, or you better understand you will only win with luck. You are not in the gambling business, so do not waste your time where you have been unable to forge strong, meaningful connections. If you are early in the sales process, then identify who will be your supporter/s and mentor and start the plan to make the powerful human connection to achieve this. Without a coach inside your customer, it is difficult to plan an effective strategy as you will be operating on either limited, or potentially erroneous, information given through guesswork, or even potentially benign, or malicious, misinformation.

As part of your strategy you will want to include how you will use the supporters and influential people to promote your solution. You will need to know how to win over, or silence, the opposers. These are the people who hate the project , the decision maker, the recommender, your company, the technology, or you. They will do whatever they can to stop you winning, as will the enemies, who are the mentors of your competitors.

You need to also understand if your selected mentor is just everyone's friend, considers themselves neutral, thus gives everyone the same information. These people are also very useful to check information, however you will usually need more support than this to win substantial projects.

Now you should make a clearly defined client political reference map, and as this is not a sales course, I am not going to tell you how to physically do that task. You should already know, otherwise do it however you can best remember it. An Organisation chart with rings, a list of names, a mind map, whatever suits your personality. The only thing I would suggest is have it written where you can refer to it, not just in your head.

I promised at the beginning, that 999 would not be a methodology, so please practice your creativity here.

When drawing up your map, the sort of questions you need to ask yourself, and perhaps others, are:

Who Can Influence The Result?

What is the coverage needed if I lose one, or more, of the influencers? Have a backup for every key influencer.

Who are my second level mentors and supporters?

Who else can I reach in the Client with other people in my own organisation?

What level of coverage do I need with each person?

Who can block me?

Who are my competitors' supporters?

Where are the Wolves and Hyenas?

Have I included the business need influencers?

Have I missed anyone who can impact me?

Make sure that every question is answered, and pay particular attention to the second question on coverage!

Be as broad as possible in your coverage. Think about your clients' financial controller, the accounting department and the supplier status of your company, and do not forget the very influential advisers - their legal liaison. You do not want to close a deal only to find the two legal teams could never agree on a standard term in a contract. I have been in many deals where the legal, or accounting, teams have had a lot of influence about which supplier is finally selected, usually based on past experience. Be aware if there is a purchasing office that will intervene at the last moment, and possibly restart price negotiations, working with them earlier is a short cut to success and a realistic close date expectation. (Define 'close' as when the contract is signed, or the PO in your hand!)

Being unaware of how every client functions in a sales process is a death knell. Look at this ridiculously simple example:

> *My partner, a friend and I walked into a large camera store, as I wanted to look at, and possibly buy, an expensive camera and accessories.*
>
> *The Sales person failed to make a connection with the buyer. I had even said "I have come in to see, and possibly buy, the Pentax 999x model." Instead he started to ask my partner questions, and tell him lots of facts that I already knew about this camera. I was an informed customer, who had completed hours of research. I was ready to make a buying decision.*
>
> *The Salesman failed to quickly outline a political reference of our small team. My partner had not been involved in the research project, so he was quite happy to be entertained with lots of information, and the salesman was happy to comply. The Salesman was therefore wasting valuable time making a wrong connection!*
>
> *Just a block away was another large camera store. Whilst my partner was engaged in information exchange with this sales person, our friend and I left and went to the second store. I was able to transact the business with a sales person who heard clearly what I said, identified the decision maker*

correctly, and we returned with the sale closed and the products in a bag. The salesperson at the first store was still busy selling to someone who was not even an influencer!

He seemed surprised when I arrived with the competitive store bag. He said ' I was still explaining everything to your friend.' My partner told him ' Thank you very much for the information, it was most interesting, and if ever I am in the market I know where to come. Today, however, I am not the buyer"

This sales person had just never bothered to find out the political reference in our team of three. He missed the sale because of this oversight, and focussed on the wrong person.

What is the purpose of this story? To demonstrate that even in the simplest sale transaction, the political reference is an essential element, to be sure you make the right human connection and never miss an opportunity. The key decision makers and influencers may not be obvious.

Covering The C Level

This is a part of every high value salespersons life. I receive probably more questions about this potentially difficult, and often treacherous path, than almost any other aspect of general sales coaching.

The C level sell can be challenging.

First how do you get there, when and with what message. Then you have the added complication of a sales process going incredibly well and your C level visit doing more damage than good.

The first step in establishing what C level person or people, you need to cover, is in clearly understanding who is interested in this decision, or if the total buying authority is delegated. Will the COO, CEO or CFO have to sign off on the deal, or the funding? Will the Board be involved?

Very accomplished sales people, and Sales Legends, are often welcome at the door of a C level client executive. Not every sales person belongs there though. If you are in that door, you better have a relevant message and the confidence to present it outstandingly, or you may be eaten alive or worse perceived as a vacuous opportunist.

If you establish that very senior people will make this decision, then you must ensure they are covered properly and well briefed.

Normally, the most appropriate way is to use your own C level.

> *In a sale with a value of over 16 million dollars into the chemical industry, it was clear that my team needed to be well represented at the level of the client CFO.*
>
> *The CEO and others would not be involved, or even probably informed, of this decision (such was the size of the company). However the CFO would be required to sign off the funding. He would be interested in knowing who this company was, for whom he was committing to such a vast amount of cash flow and investment.*
>
> *We arranged for our CFO to fly to the USA, from Europe, to*

meet with the client CFO. We decided, as part of our strategy, that no sales person would go, as the CFO had a delicate task to achieve.

Our competitors had placed a strong rumour within the client that our company, the then preferred solution, was likely to be bankrupt within six months. The tough part was, it could have been true! We were in trouble with cash, and struggling to keep doors opened. Although business was still running very well, we had losses sustained in previous years that had depleted cash. Every deal we closed was a delicate act of balancing special support from our suppliers.

Our CFO was very nervous, as he did not consider himself a salesperson and was afraid he would make a mistake. We coached him extensively, even with role plays, and then sent him off on his plane with our confidence. We believed that if no sales person was in the room, he would perform better at a CFO to CFO level.

He did the trick! He was able to convince the CFO of the client that although things were tough, we had appropriate arrangements in place financially, that would ensure the project was delivered efficiently. He was able to articulate all the reasons why we would not go bankrupt, but instead trade out of difficulty. Our strategy was right, because maybe he could not have gained the confidence of the client CFO with a sales person present.

And, Yes, of course we won!

You will see from this example, that it may not only be important that your own C level people engage the C level of the client, but that you must consider even if you should be present.

Sometimes in a room with two CEOs, I have witnessed the sales person feeling uncomfortable because he, or she ,is being spoken down to by the client CEO. Then possibly your own CEO feels a need to defend your honour, and a sticky situation ensues. There is no excuse for bad manners in a CEO, but there is no room for a sales person to let ego get in the way of their sales process either!

Sometimes a client CEO will impart information to a fellow C level colleague, that you would never receive as a sales person. This information can be your golden bullet to winning against all odds.

Who to send, and at what times in the sales process, to whom in your client, will be a decision you have to make in line with your strategy.

If you are doing this all yourself, and you are having trouble getting in the door of the client C level, then you must ask yourself - why are you there?

You need a compelling reason for them to see you. Realistically, they do not have time to see every supplier, about every deal, so why you?

You will have to convince an, often very protective, assistant that your reason is compelling enough – else the C level executive may never even know you tried. Sometimes, you can use your chain of influence, as evidenced on your political reference map to open the door for you. Be careful though, as they need to be in his personal inner circle, or else their introduction may have the reverse effect than you desire.

Once you have some minutes in the esteemed presence of the client C level, you will need to use everything we have discussed so far, to ensure that the meeting is a success.

You need to make a great human connection. Then you need to make that executive feel comfortable and deliver a flawless, and in their opinion relevant, message. You must be on time, and finish in time. Do not bore them with slides unless entirely appropriate. Be sure your messaging is at the appropriate business level, and do not attempt to entertain him, or her, with your knowledge of the bells and whistles of your solution, unless they ask you to. Speak only of business benefit relevant to that client.

Remember, be careful when using common ground with a C level executive as he, or she, may not actually give a shit!! Any common ground better be business based, non competitive to their business, non threatening and very strongly connected. Be very careful using their competitors as a subject, they probably know more about them than you do.

If you can use relevant reference from a member of his team, that may be powerful.

> *'John Williams (the VP of engineering) suggested I ask you for this time, as he was concerned that you be in a strong position to fully brief the Board next week on solutions for the new plant. John thought I may be able to answer any concerns you have in advance....etc.*

Be unafraid to ask meaningful and open questions at the C level, or to ask your representative to do so. It is a good opportunity to verify what this final decision maker thinks about your strategy, your solution, your finance proposal or anyone else they would like to see you brief in their organisation. He may save your butt by telling you, or your representative, that there is something you failed to cover off!

Relevancy, timing, and appropriate person for the contact are the key pre-requisites to consider before any C level meeting takes place.

A precaution to note, when selling to government. Be very careful using people like Ministers directly. Sometimes such a visit can be politically twisted in a compromise, and cause you to lose a deal. It is better to use experienced lobbyists for such tasks, unless you happen to know someone who is close to the Minister who can recommend you and your solution without compromising that relationship, or you.

Be prepared to invest time, or ask your C level to invest time, in forming good connections with client C level. Ideally this time should not be perceived to be related to a specific deal but benefit the company overall.

> *Two colleagues of mine were locked head to head in Asia, in a very large telecommunications deal.*
>
> *One colleague, Sean, an excellent salesman, was confident he would win because he won the technical evaluation, and had the better price! I advised him that he had a formidable opponent, as my other colleague was truly a great Sales*

Legend, who would be fully aware he was on the back foot.

My other colleague, Mac, as expected had political bases well covered. He also had an excellent professional relationship with the CEO of the Telco.. They had met socially at the golf club, and regularly played together. This colleague never needed to do the 'C level' official visit, the CEO was well aware of who he was.

The week before the decision day, Mac played golf with the client CEO. On the 5th hole, just before teeing off, the CEO said to Mac, "I know you are involved in the infrastructure deal inside my company, but I wanted to be honest and tell you I am sorry I don't think I can do a lot to help you, the technical team seem to really favour the other solution.'

Mac took his shot, and then looked at the CEO and said "Actually I agree with your technical team that the other company has a great new generation solution at a great price. They offer new features that we have not yet incorporated. This is an attractive proposition. The only additional consideration I would have in your place, is that new technology is not so tried and proven, and whilst the company is leading edge and visionary, it is still young and small. As part of your critical service offering, if something goes wrong, I guess you need to know that whoever is behind you is very sound with a proven technology and an experienced team. I do not envy you having to make the final decision, it is a tough one."

They carried on playing, and the subject was never raised

again. Such is the long term strategy, human connection and subtlety of a Sales Legend.

The following week, Mac's company was awarded the contract!

The CEO made a risk averse, and relationship based decision.

The C level is critical, but it is even more critical to execute any contact with excellence, and in line with an overall strategy for the client.

Buyer Motivation

We learnt way back in Sales 101, that buyers are motivated primarily by their own needs. We understand that whilst the business needs must be met, most competitors that bid for a solution can meet that basic requirement, or they really are idiots who will be discounted in the evaluation process.

So what differentiates the best, from the average sales person here?

It is the depth of understanding of what will motivate and influence each buyer in the decision tree. What personal needs do they have that should be satisfied in this sale process?

Buyers may have many needs at the subconscious level that need to be met. You could consider the following:

Risk Minimisation - Need for preservation of role, or job

In other words, they are going to be unlikely to want to make any decision that is risky, if it has exposure or high value. They may want to make it someone else's' decision of which they only executed the PO. Alternatively, they may make you sell it all over again just to their team. They may avoid a risky decision altogether.

This means you will need to minimise this buyers risk at all times, and reassure them that a decision to use your solution will be a safe one.

Years ago there used to be an expression ' Nobody gets fired for buying IBM'.

As a new technology company, often in competition with IBM, this had the potential to send a salesperson nuts!

It meant that as a buyer, if you took the safe route, of proven technology, backed by a huge company then no one could be blamed if anything went wrong.

If the project went poorly, and someone screamed 'who made this decision and why?'

A Buyer could confidently say "I made the decision, and I chose the proven performer with a lot of experience" It was difficult to lay blame on them.

If you had to say "I chose the latest bleeding edge technology, at a better price" but the project was delayed and a business application affected – you could be considered having made a rash decision and promptly fired.

Fortunately, there were enough competent sales people around to overcome this resistance from buyers and today there are a wider range of safe choices in technology!.

Recognition – Buyer may seek promotion or a different role

In this case, the buyer will be motivated by anything that will make them look really good to his superiors, or senior colleagues. What can you as a sales person deliver to this buyer that will assist him, or her, fulfil this need? Perhaps they like meeting influential people, and you have someone appropriate in your company with a suitable title to meet and impress upon your decision maker their importance to your company.

Are there company events appropriate to invite your buyer, that will make them feel a sense of importance and prestige. An event they can tell their colleagues about.

Can you retain a small buying point that ensures they did something extra or special, they negotiated an extra concession of value, thus justifying their decision. Perhaps you can tell their colleagues how thorough they were in a positive context, and how they are one of your most challenging clients because of their expertise.

Desire for Prestige

Some buyers find it difficult to select a supplier that does not offer a feeling of exclusivity and prestige. A feeling they have bought the best, they only associate with the best.

You will need to consider ways to show that you recognise that this buyer is a man, or woman, of prestige and importance. You may no longer shower them with expensive gifts or entertainment, or you will both end up in a non-prestigious place indeed, but you can ensure that any business proposal you give them reeks of a top line professional presentation. If you bring cakes for morning tea for their team, bring them from a gourmet bakery and not the local

Dunkin' Donuts! Show their team you respect this is a person of some standing, metaphorically enforcing their need for prestige.

You must find out what is important to your buyer personally. What need must they satisfy when they make their decision? It will rarely be solely about choosing the best solution for the business needs. There are a myriad of political, and personal, agendas hidden away in every decision maker that you can use to advance your chances of closing a sale.

You can consider other motivations like social connection, importance of family, sport, hobbies and interests.

Let us just look at the simple art of buying a new suit. Think about the last time you bought a suit.

Ask yourself why you chose the one you did, from the shop you did. Not all good sales people are also good buyers, it is the reverse art of selling, but we love to be sold to. We absolutely subconsciously delight in the event of another sales person actually uncovering our buying motivation, and personal needs, and closing us on them.

So, why did you buy that suit, from that shop? Identify your own real decision criteria and see how it was met. Did you pay more than you intended, because your needs were met? Did that seller make a great connection with you? Will you return there next time you need a suit?

> *At the risk of having you decide I am shallow and ego-centric, I am going to briefly share some personal motivations to help you further understand this concept.*

When I buy a suit I like to feel a mix of seductive power and prestige when I try it on!

My real decision criteria is when I look in that mirror and think 'I can win' in this suit!

So I am an ego pacifying buyer. It is all about my image and ego.

I am less influenced by price, although I love a bargain, I am more likely to be able to justify the extra if I feel the way I want to feel. I know this feeling helps me sell more! So I will earn more, therefore I can afford it.

I will be less impressed by durability, or fabric performance, at the time of purchase. If it crushes in the car, I will forgive it and not blame the seller.

It is all about the feel of the fabric, the colour of the lining in a jacket and the look of the cut. It is an emotional decision, even in a person as practical as I am! The person I like to buy from sells to that ego and inner desire to be powerful. They do not say ' It is pretty' or 'Sexy' or 'Cute' or that it is a bargain, or wash and wear.

When I select food items I am influenced by anything that appears to be gourmet. I prefer it packaged in glass with a wax and fabric seal, rather than plastic with a vacuum lid. A handwritten, or antique style label. An association with a region known for the best.

I appreciate good service, and I am a lamb for slaughter in the hands of a great sales person who recognises all this, and sells to it.

It is less about what others think, and more about how good it makes me feel, and if it pleases my eye and fits my image of me.

A very simple exercise like this, about yourself, will help you understand how to identify faster the personal needs of your customers, apart from the practical decision criteria. Meet these needs and you are progressing quickly in both human connection and your sales process.

Identify both the business and personal motivations and needs of your decision makers and sell to meet those needs.

If you sell to the buyers, not the company, (remember a company is not a decision making entity) you will sell more and you will sell with ease!

Hard Line Qualification

Hard Line Qualification

A Sales Legend will know with a high degree of certainty whether or not they can, and will, win a deal. This comes partly from experience, but mostly this is the result of a 'knowing' that they have followed all the elements of a great sales campaign or not.

From these elements comes a full understanding of the client business case, appropriate coverage at all influential points within the client and a level of connection that will mean he or she is alerted to any change however minor.

They will be sure that everyone on their own virtual team has followed up, and done their part towards the closing step. They will have silver and gold bullets ready if required, they will have spread goodwill and good business sense everywhere. They will have planned to win!

It all begins with a very hard look whether it is even possible to win this client and/or this deal. You will be aware of what can stop you, and have a plan to neutralise any negative influences.

It is possible to predict with reliability whether you can, or will, win a deal or a client.

In the heat of the excitement of a new deal or client to enter in the CRM, truly honest qualification is frequently overlooked, and we waste valuable resources, time and energy chasing something we will never have. Dream chasing, instead of objective rational sales process.

This is happening everywhere, and it is wasting company resources, draining profitability and frustrating salespeople. Even very experienced salespeople very rarely spend sufficient time and energy in the qualification phase.

So no apologies about telling you 'how to suck eggs', because more than 95% of you still need to get this vital step absolutely right! If you do, you can expect to win 85% of your bids!

Am I a day late, or a dollar short?

How long have you known about this opportunity? Did you find the RFP in a newspaper, or were you there before the project was even conceived? If you were not, then your chances of winning are indeed quite low.

There are a few rare exceptions:

- You have a unique technology with a perfect client fit, when no one else has, and your client was unaware you existed until the last few weeks before buying a solution. The customer invited you to bid.

- It is a secret organisation where you are well connected, but they do not announce any opportunity prior to the release of an RFI. However, you better be very well connected and if you are I would suggest that the smell of an impending project would have reached your nostrils!
- It is a price only deal, less than 1% of deals.
- Something else that is rare and unique, that I cannot think of right now!

The only winners of large solution deals are those who are trusted by the client and who have put in the hard yards to win the race.

The rest of you, despite what you are told, are just there for price comparison or it is an open tender by law, or for interest only.

This is a time for honesty and integrity. If you are not well placed, then how the hell are you going to be able to overtake all the other runners and cross the line. If you just said price, I may kill you!

That is the next part of my question above. Are you going to be able to price your solution to justify value and be competitive? That does not mean be the cheapest. What weighting does price have in the selection process?

> *As Senior VP of Global Operations and Sales for a high end solutions provider, we were not in business for market share we were only there for profitable, long term business.*
>
> *In this case, we were not even interested in short term gain strategies for long term business. i.e. Get the first order then up the ante for a subsequent bigger deal, after proving ourselves.*
>
> *I used to ask CIOs on the very first presentation and information gathering meeting how important price was, telling them we would not be the cheapest but we would demonstrate we could be the best value for money.*
>
> *The answer from the decision maker, sometimes meant that we thanked them for the opportunity but advised we would not be bidding as we could not win. These CIOs were often very grateful for our honesty and referred us to colleagues.*
>
> *The decision makers who advised us not to worry about not being the cheapest, had just solved the problem. We had just*

set an expectation that we could meet – pay a bit more – get a lot more value.

These first two questions may well quickly identify what time and resource, if any, you should invest in a given client or opportunity.

In that same solutions provider, I once had to explain to the Board, why I had blocked a key sales wolf from bidding an opportunity worth 6 million dollars into a huge defence organisation where we already had good relationships and existing business.

I explained that it was because we would not win, and why.

The Board not only approved my decision, but went on to promote me into a bigger role as they were extremely impressed with the pragmatism and business rationale that had just saved the company at least $100,000 on a bid we clearly could not win. The Chairman commented he had not seen a presentation like this before. Instead those resources were committed to business we could profitably win and did!

Interestingly, the next time I met the client, he asked me 'I am curious, why didn't you bid?' I told him the truth, He said 'You are absolutely right you would never have won and I really respect your decision, it saved me a lot of additional time and angst, and your company a lot of money and distraction.'

He then went on to say that there was a new project I should be looking at, and referred me to the right person with an introduction. It was a bigger project that we could win!

How and Why Am I In?

If your opportunity passed the first two tests, you should now spend some time understanding how and why you are in this sales process, be it a new opportunity or a new client.

You are not lucky and it is not because you were assigned that client. Go up a few notches on the strategy scale. How did you find out about this opportunity? Do you already have a good existing relationship with at least some of the key influencers? Did they call you and tell you about this? Were you invited to a meeting with a senior executive who invited you to become involved to help him or her? (Now you have my attention)

What right do you have to win this opportunity? Make sure you can clearly articulate this to yourself and your support team. If they understand why you are there, then they will have stronger faith in your ability to execute a great winning campaign.

How and Why you are there is a very valuable piece of information to consider in planning your strategy.

Can We Win?

This is a time to realistically assess your company, and their ability to deliver on your promises. Consider resourcing before and after the close, are those resources available to you in a timely and effective manner?

Do you have a solution that is an exact match to meet your clients requirements? Can you value add on top of this basic match? How does your solution compare to your competitors? Can you even do what's required, or are you needing partnerships to meet the full specifications? Will this advantage or disadvantage you?

Do you have the technology? the services to implement? the products?

Evaluate each element of your proposed solution and understand how you will position it not only to win, but to disadvantage your competition. Analyse thoroughly to know whether or not you have the winning solution around which you can wrap intelligent strategy and unbeatable value.

Are there already strong relationships in place? Yours or Others? Are you the incumbent supplier or do you have to oust another? Does your client need to throw away investments made in alternate solutions that are still on the books at value? What is their real cost of ownership, what is the ROI and can you sell this to advantage?

Can we win? The answer lies in integrity of solution, strength of relationship and how effective your strategy will be.

In the event of a high value deal, or huge customer, then pay more attention. This should be in a brainstorm room with the team that you would select to support your offer. Include finance, legal, operations, another sales person, and ask your Sales Leader to play the role of the decision maker afterwards, and try to bring you unstuck!

Will We Win? Why?

Now that you have decided you *can* win, you need to fully understand if you *will* win. What is the difference?

Well the fact that you can win, does not mean that you will win!

Can, is about your abilities as a company, a team and a salesperson to offer a winning solution that will beat your competition.

Will, is a step further. So I can win because I have everything I need to provide a great solution, but who can knock me out and why can they? Analyse all potential competitors carefully, look at both their strengths and weaknesses, and then ascertain if you can match their strengths yet use their weaknesses against them. Determine which of your likely competitors will represent your biggest threats.

What price will you have to pay to win? Think here of resource commitment, discounts, packaged offer, sacrifice of attention on other clients and deals and personal energy cost. Be certain you can pay the price.

Analyse market and environmental conditions. Study political ramifications, they can defeat you before you start and sometimes be unchangeable.

> *For example in some cooperative environments, the client does not like to see the same country win all the business even if they are the best solution at a great price. They have in their charter, an agreement that all host countries will share the business on a rotational basis, and this may carry up to a 50% weighting in the decision criteria. This is an unchangeable parameter, and unless you have a formidable strategy on how you will get around this and survive the flack of the aftermath, might as well go find a piece of business less resource intensive, and more cost effective, to win. Winning at all costs is not the stuff of Legends!*

Once you have determined you *will* win, you can now commit

yourself to the following steps, and they are less likely to hold you back. Once you are committed remember that all manner of unforseen events will take place, that you could not have imagined before, to help you close the deal.

To be sure you are committed, present your reasons why you will win to a good strategist and ask them to be devils' advocate for you.

Qualification is one of the most important steps in the sales process.

Now you have a commitment that you can and will win if you proceed, it is time to analyse the additional parts of this opportunity.

What Risks Are There?

What could go wrong? Look at your worst case scenarios. What if the CEO is fired or leaves. What if the demonstration does not go perfectly? What if the competitor drops a piece of information you would prefer to have kept private in front of the client? What if the competitor releases a hot, new technology? Is there any customisation?

Again look at every possible angle barring World War 3 breaking in that country or a massive natural disaster.

> *Although there was one qualification process where I was coach for the bid team. They actually ascertained that in the event of a natural disaster there would be an even more compelling reason to go ahead with the project – an upgrade in technology!*

You should consider environmental impact such as elections. An election can have an impact on a major project, dependant on where the client gains their business, their funding source, or on which party they rely for business benefits. Perhaps a particular party taking power would impact this client to the point they change suppliers, or cancel projects.

> *My colleague, Junior, was selling a large commercial estate to a developer. An impending election could have had catastrophic effects as planning permissions may have been revoked for this controversial project, or it may have influenced which piece of land this developer then bought.*

What Strategy Will Win?

At this time, we do not need to plan our strategy, but we must understand whether we can choose and implement what is required for a winning strategy, including all the Plan B's in the event of possible changes along the way. Take out your crystal ball here and try to imagine what could happen along the timeline of the sales process. Can you implement a strategy and a back up to ensure that your commitment to winning will be unaffected?

Do you have access to the resources to implement this strategy? Maybe you need to ensure that the right people will be available as and when you need them.

> *Kirk forgot that last point. He had implemented a fairly brilliant strategy, that needed the Chairman of the Board of his company to play a certain role for definite closure. The Chairman, he knew, was always willing to help Kirk in high level strategy like this.*

However, Kirk did not ascertain early enough that his Chairman would be available. Normally a few days here and there would not matter, but the Chairman was scheduled for major surgery in a few weeks and would be out of service for at least 6-8 weeks.

There was no plan B, there was not even a 'what if' in the event such a situation occurred.

Work out what type of strategy you are going to need to win and then ensure you have the resources (finance, approvals, people, design etc) available to implement it. Are you allowed in your organisation to implement a strategy like this? No point in a killer strategy if someone waves a governance credo in front of you at a critical point!

Full Resource Analysis

By now you know you can and will win. You know why you will win, that you can and will pay the price of winning, and what risks you are exposed to. You have an idea of the type of strategic plan you need to win and believe it is doable. You are almost there, but there are a couple of important steps before committing everything and putting 100% focus into winning this opportunity.

You need to now analyse what resources you are going to need to win, and then what resources you will need within the first few months after closing the deal. Are you and your organisation ready?

Do you have access to enough time from the key people that you need on your virtual support team? What are their workloads like at the critical times in your forthcoming sales campaign?

When you win, will you need a project manager? Who will be available? Is it possible to involve them prior to closing the sale? If they are a great project manager, they can contribute heavily to your sales campaign adding a sense of reality and credibility. A decision already made – and here is the Project Manager!

Will the administrative support be available if there is a Response to Tender required? You need to analyse your resource pool very thoroughly and be sure the people you can work with will be available when you need them. You will not want any nasty surprises along the way, such as your favourite in house corporate lawyer, the one who helped you win before is committed elsewhere and you are left with the lawyer for whose abilities and time management, you have less faith. You do not want to be let down, and if you are going to commit to winning, then resource availability is significant at this time.

Regarding post sale resource – why would you bother, the Purchase Order is in the bag? Most companies do not pay your commission until revenue is recognised, or at least invoiced! So if you make a legendary sale and cannot start on the projected date, then you delay revenue recognition, and your commission!

Competitive Analysis

When you were agonising over whether you could win, and would win, you looked at your competitors strengths and weaknesses.

Take those out again now, and undergo a thorough analysis of what their campaign is likely to look like. Include elements like strategy, selling style, competitive advantage, and timing of what they are likely to do and when.

Ensure you have coverage for every likely scenario they could roll out. How will you turn their strengths into a plus for you, and how will you use their weakness against them in a subtle yet deadly way?

How are they likely to see your strengths and weaknesses and what will they do to capitalise on these?

If you are sure you have the ground to cover your competitors, and are still convinced you can and will win, then it is time for the final step.

What Could Stop Me Winning?

This is your last critical question to answer for you to be able to commit everything you have to winning this deal, client or opportunity.

When you run your opportunity past your Leader, your teams, ask everyone this question so you are always sure, on a daily basis, you have everything covered. Get ready to think on your feet from the day you commit to winning, and move forward confidently.

Ask this question of yourself in the bath, before bed and sleep on it, driving in the car. Meditate on this question! Hopefully, you do not find any answers or any surprises, but if you do then at least you will not blindly walk on following your original plan, but instead react swiftly and effectively like a laser beam to remove the obstacle or objection!

If you got this far, with an opportunity, then the only thing left that could lose you this sale is being outsold! That, at least, you can respect and learn from. However, if you follow the path of a Legend, you are very unlikely to be outsold more than a few times in a lot of years.

> *Remember, back in the Political Reference we looked briefly at a case study of Sean and Mac, my two colleagues selling a very large solution. You may recall that Mac won, and he did outsell Sean.*
>
> *However, Sean left the door open for that to have happened, it was not a fait accompli. Had he recognised in his qualification phase, when he analysed his competitors likely sales campaign, his weakness and Macs strength. Then he would have guessed that Mac would use the strength of company position as a final strategic position, and Sean could have taken steps to proactively neutralise a comment like Mac made on the golf course.*
>
> *Sean could have still won!*

As an interesting exercise, how would you have built in a safe guard against that positioning of strength? It is not even so difficult as remember Sean, had a very strong position!

Make sure you always have these answers ready, so that anything that could stop you winning is effectively neutralised. Later, you will learn the secret of the golden bullet and that will also assist you.

This qualification process is lengthy, should not be rushed and you should take a very harsh line. Most sales are won or lost at this time – poor qualification is a time and resource waster, sets good people (including yourself) up for disappointment and energy loss and of course diffuses your focus. It can also cost you your ranking on the sales ladder or even your job. It is a gift for your good competitors. If they are going to win anyway why bother putting up a fight? It is better to go get something else, than stay in a battle you know you will lose.

An expectation of loss, or a hesitation in commitment, will rarely see a surprise win! Qualify Hard, Bid Less and Win More!

Sales People Tip:

At this qualifying stage, once you are sure you can win, you should take some time to negotiate your commission and have that resolved in writing. Many companies have a comp plan where any deal over a certain size becomes exempt and subject to negotiation.

> *I have seen a major distraction entering the sales process near the closing phase. The Salesperson began to hear rumblings of the commission likely to be paid, that it would be less than half the normal plan. In fact he even heard that it could be a fixed fee, which was quite low.*

> *It would mean he would have achieved 250% of target but only receive 120% in commission. This became very stressful for the salesperson, and naturally they began to spend more time trying to fix a fair payment of commission than focus on their client and the sale process, they almost lost the sale. Everyone became involved, gossiping about it, and becoming de-motivated. It was a mess. This is not the first time I have seen this.*

Resolve any likely commission issues now!

Sales Leaders Caution:

If you ignore this compensation issue now, it **will** bite you in the bum later, and may cost you the sale. A de-motivated, or distracted salesperson is only operating at best around 50% of potential.

You cannot afford this.

If you have a large deal exception commission plan, then please negotiate early, or pay full commission later!

Focus

Focus

Sales Legends are incredibly focussed. Not just on winning the deal but on exploring new business within the client, thus simultaneously developing their future and enhancing the client relationship. They are also appropriately focussed on their personal affairs, thus living a relatively well organised and stress minimised life.

Again, we need to take a holistic view of focus to ensure a good life balance for the busy sales executive. To maximise effectiveness everywhere in your life, you need to be focussed on what is important at that moment in time. You need a clear vision and understanding that your priorities are in the right order, and that they take place of focus at the appropriate time. Simply put – when at work focus on work, when at sport focus on the sport, when at home your focus is on family, friends and relaxation.

Your order of priority needs to be adjusted according to where you are, so for example at home your first priority should be your family and relaxation but a second priority is your work, as they can sometimes overlap even with the best laid plans of mice and men! You need to be able to switch quickly from one to another, and back. This way you will minimise stress, and overload.

At work your priority must be work, your client and sales process and unless it is an emergency, or an important occasion that will impact your life if you do not give attention.

> *You forgot your wife's birthday, it is noon and you have to cancel a meeting to rectify your problem. Otherwise, your life will be hell for another year at least!*

> *This is excusable unless the meeting was critical, and then you are in a hell of a place, you have to choose which side of hell looks worse!!*

Think I just proved my point about the holistic organisation you see in a Sales Legends life!

I know colleagues who have needed to excuse themselves from a meeting for an important call on their gsm.

It was not their wife going into labour, or their husband had an accident, it was simply something like an enquiry about which colour paint should be selected at the store for the kitchen.

Now that is an example of loss of focus. What was the gsm doing on during a meeting? (Unless there was an urgent situation brewing) and the paint decision should wait until that evening. A Sales Legend will have arranged that the paint decision was made the previous evening, and the colour sample attached to a paper for their partner to select.

Hopefully, in a light hearted way, you can see what I mean by appropriate priorities and focus. Without this focus your work will overlap into your personal space everyday and that will cause you problems and stress. Your personal life will weave its way in and out of your work day, distracting you from winning and again causing stress.

People without the ability to appropriately prioritise and focus are the ones who usually burn out.

Now we will explore some key elements of priority setting and focus.

What Do I Need To Change In My Life?

Is your personal life a bit of a mess, or do you have it well organised so it rarely interrupts your work day? Is your work life managed so that it rarely interferes with your personal time?

This is important for high achievers. It prevents burn out, it maintains energy, minimises stress and keeps you motivated.

Track your average day, try selecting last Tuesday. What was last Tuesday like? Were there many distractions that stopped you achieving your expectations for that day, or that caused stress? Run through this day in your head and see how you would ideally like it to have run. Analyse the gaps and then look at how you need to refocus your attention, so that you get your desired daily run.

If you are quite chaotic, or struggling to manage everything then I suggest you buy a copy of *30 Days of Inspiration*. This is a book I wrote specifically to help people get their life ready for success. If you follow the suggestions for each day, at the end of a month you could well be astonished at how much smoother your life runs. It also helps you manage stress and even conflict situations, much more effectively.

Do you still need a time management course to help you regain some focus? Everyone of you will have different needs.

The essential thing is to do something, and do it now. If you do not, then you will never be really successful in a sustainable way.

It is possible to arrange your life that, barring emergencies, you will be able to have your attention on the correct ball at all times. You will be able then to ensure you have a clear distinction between work and play, although applying many of the same habits and skills to both situations. This will keep up your energy levels and help you bounce into each and every day full of the passion and enthusiasm that you need to win. To win your sales, to win at sport, and to win with family and friends.

As a guide to helping yourself, look at things like how you are organised – how much time and energy do you have to expend looking for things? Are you avoiding, or minimising by managing your reactions, as much conflict in work and play as possible?

Learn to use techniques like:

Reframing – the ability to look at the world in a more appealing way.

Visualisation – clearly seeing in your mind what it is that you desire, and keeping that mental picture to hand with either vision boards, or on a screensaver, or just mentally recalling the picture several times a day.

Vision Boards – A board, or collection of visual representations of that which you are working for, or needing to materialise. Have them where you see them every day. Remember the impact of 680 that we discussed as part of The Law of Attraction.

Personal Goal Setting - ten personal Goals per year, every year, and committing them to paper. We will revisit this again, later in this chapter.

Handling Patterns for Email – email is one of the greatest distracters and time wasters in our day. Yet it is also a critical communications tool, so we must manage it so that we can focus only on the important things. I have included some basic tips, in the final chapter, that cover email handling. It is a problem that plagues even the most senior people, yet it is not impossible to manage.

Same Place – Assign places to put things that are similar. Examples could include an In tray for all snail mail received, that needs attention later; a cupboard dedicated to sporting gear; a place for everything to be, even approximately (if you are unwilling, like me, to be a perfectionist) is good enough. If you know that all sports gear is in rear left corner of your garage, then it takes only a minute to locate the skis you last used six months ago.

Probably sounds a bit anally retentive, but actually it gives you back hours a week and you are free of frustration from small things. You no longer spend time searching for things. The average person spends more than 60 minutes a day on this, to me, very frustrating task!

Families get into arguments about lost things, blame flies like a giant seagull and ill feeling depletes quality of life and energy.

Diary Time – Set time aside formally in your diary every day for returning less critical calls, managing emails, and unexpected actions. Learn to put everything in your agenda, personal and work, so you can see the important expectations of your day and week at a glance.

Emotional Management – We cannot control everything that happens in our lives, but we have 100% control over how we react to it. By remaining calm, (try breathing techniques) and being able to think clearly in every circumstance, our performance as a human and as a salesperson will be greatly enhanced. If you allow too much emotion to control your reactions, then you will be very stressed and unable to respond as effectively. Even in an emergency, a highly emotional reaction will not help anyone, least of all you.

I could quote you thousands of examples of stressful situations made worse by a salesperson losing their cool. Deals lost, clients alienated, suppliers support withdrawn, team members walking out at a critical time and every other disaster you can think of – caused by the salesperson not being in emotional control.

Punch a wall later if you need, but stay calm and rational in front of your team and the customer at all times. It is possible to appear tougher, nicer, more amenable, more considered, more remote, warmer, colder – all emotions can be even better expressed through a state of apparent calm.

My Asian colleagues call it 'Stone Face' – do not expose your weakness, or your strength, through your emotions and expressions.

Enigmatic people, who are still personable and charismatic are the most fascinating people to observe. They receive an extraordinary amount of positive attention!

> *This reminds me of a Truly Great Leader, to whom I had the privilege of reporting as a young Sales Leader.*
>
> *He once saw me hurrying along the corridor to a meeting. He stopped me in my tracks, placed his hand on my shoulder to steady me, and said ' Terrie, a few small words of wisdom for you, as a Senior Manager: Never run. It panics the troops!'*
>
> *Now, I have to tell you Hans was one of the most inspirational CEOs I have ever worked with. He had the aura of a man of significance, yet the manners of a gentleman at*

> *all times. He never raised his voice, yet when he spoke he commanded the attention of all around him. He didn't need to hear the sound of his own voice, he was a searching questioner and an engaged listener. He never displayed a lot of emotion, yet you knew when he was displeased, but there was no loss of face for anyone involved. Nothing to repair but your mistake.*
>
> *He imparted an enormous amount of fast tracked knowledge for a young, up and coming executive. He truly deserved respect as an Iconic Leader of Industry.*

Hans understood the importance of non-emotional management, in creating a more productive and less stressful environment. He never worked excessive hours, he had a wonderful lifestyle, he achieved year on year and rarely appeared stressed.

Now that you have taken a holistic look at your patterns of behaviour, you have the opportunity to practise these techniques until you are satisfied that all parts of your life serve to support each other. You can prevent burn out with great focus on the appropriate priority - a win win position in all matters.

Planning and Documentation

A Sales Legend will have strong planning, goal setting and documentation skills. Do not panic, and turn off, by documentation I do not mean you will write large detailed documents! This is not a methodology remember, this is a coaching guide. You do it how you want, but I suggest if you want to stay employed stick within your company guidelines.

Planning should be a high priority in your life. You are a very busy person, who wants to maximise their effectiveness, and likely fit more in your day than the average person in a week. Let's consider here what sort of plans you need to have, and how to do them without feeling too controlled.

Annual Plans

There are two kinds of annual plans I would expect a top salesperson to have.

First he, or she, needs a plan for their life goals. I recommend that every year, at the same time you write a list of the ten most important things you want to achieve in the coming year. You consider your list, and when satisfied you have chosen your correct goals (remember we usually get what we commit to) then decide if you need to make any visual boards, or other kinds of reminders. Now put your piece of paper away in a safe place where you will find it again next year. Do not neglect to write your goals down.

Experience has proven that if you commit on paper, then you will achieve 7-10 of your goals. If you do not, you are likely to achieve on average 2-3!

Being a bit of a sceptic in the early days, I needed to prove to myself that the results were as my mentor had indicated. They were. Now, I never neglect this simple act of commitment every year and I am delighted with my results.

Next you need an annual business development plan for your major clients. This plan should include all the basic information that would be handed to a new salesperson in event you are hit by a bus. This is just a matter of good account management. You should always have up to date client organisation charts and political reference maps.

A list of active competitors in this account with short overview of their strengths and weaknesses.

Ideally it would include summary of the previous years' business, preferably up to 5 years of brief history. The previous year page should outline major sales campaigns won and lost, and any brickbats or bouquets, traps that were discovered etc.

It should also contain the business development plan for this coming year. This should include what projects are upcoming, what areas are marked for expansion or development, and what resources are needed. It of course should all lead to an expectation of revenue from that source. Have someone act as your devils' advocate on this plan, to identify any holes, misconceptions and assumptions.

A safe version of this development plan, without strategic content and personal commentary, should be made available for discussion with your client and mutual signoff. This is a great way to get a subliminal commitment.

Now that you have both personal and client plans for the year, you are in a good position to plan your agenda (including early acknowledgement of significant personal events). If they are in your agenda you are in a better position to avoid disappointment and stress, nor will you hopefully have to choose which side of hell looks best!

You need to plan your sales campaigns, detail your strategies and actions, and diarise as much as possible, as early as you can. If you use an electronic diary then ensure you have a hand held device ready, or a print out of your calendar at all times. Your client will not appreciate having to wait several minutes whilst you open an electronic device, to confirm an event.

You are now prepared and ready to go win, win and win again!

Ensure your plan is kept up to date, and relevant information is entered into your companys' CRM or Sales system.

Daily Running List

I am not a highly organised person by nature, but I cannot bear to waste time by having to look for things or forgetting things. I hate having to apologise when I could so easily have avoided a negative situation. I hate getting stressed because I am late before I even leave home, or worse realise that I am wearing two different black shoes! If you are smiling now, it has probably happened to you too – odd socks? keys to the wrong car? GPS is flat? Suit pocket torn, but you forgot, and now you lost the change for the bus!

As a result, I always do two simple things every day:

1. I carry a running priority list in a small pocketbook. This is my list of To Dos for today and sometimes on other week days if there is a deadline to meet. Each day I cross off what I have done, a satisfying and rewarding feeling, and then if anything is missed I add it to tomorrows' list. At times of pressure, I prioritise my list to be sure the essentials get done. This means my mind can relax after work, as it has all been recorded on the fly. If you keep a written diary, it can be in your diary, but as I use Google calendar as my diary and personal assistant, I use a notebook instead.

2. I check my list each evening, and think about what I need to wear tomorrow. What image do I need to achieve my goal list, who am I meeting etc? I also plan what time I need to

leave and set alarm accordingly. This also prevents me doing a stupid 3am bar close, when my daily list shows I have a priority task to perform early tomorrow. I then locate the clothing I plan to wear, check it for any issues (ironed, clean, repaired etc) I match up shoes and accessories, and check that everything I need is in my bag.

Why the night before?

I sleep better. I will not waken suddenly at 2am thinking, "oh crap, I mustn't forget that diagram" etc. Also I have a nice morning, no nasty surprises when I find something unironed, or can't find the correct shoes, or they need cleaning! I start my day on time, with my coffee and a smooth, calm persona. This sets me up to be in top gear to perform! ....and very focussed on the priority at hand.

I have seen people severely underperform because they were late out the door, missed their breakfast, almost had an accident enroute and then arrived at a key event flustered and stressed at 8am!! Then they regale everyone at the meeting with their tale of a bad morning in the life of salesperson x. Their drama spreads negativity and lowers the energy in a room. What hope do they have for the rest of the day but to hope it gets better!

Another quick tip, when you are at the critical phases of large sales, it is a great idea to keep pen and pad beside your bed. Sometimes great ideas come only when we have got our conscious mind to shut up – i.e. we are asleep! It is very stressful if you cannot write it down and go quickly back to sleep. First, you worry you will forget and prohibit sleep, then finally exhaustion takes over and you can awaken not to recall what your brilliant thought was!

Ensuring you have a simple plan to maximise the benefit and energy expended on a daily basis will help you retain motivation, higher energy levels and make keeping focus on what your priorities are very simple.

Note Taking

It is a great benefit to take notes at all your meetings. This should be in a notebook form, not electronic unless you are dealing with the Z generation, who may tolerate it well. Electronic note taking can appear as not paying attention, or even distract your audience.

A small notebook is fine, no need for copious notes unless you have a crap memory. Normally if you just note down key names, important prompts for information, numbers are significant so note them, and of course essential is any actions agreed with timeframes attached. This then means you can follow up accurately and in a timely manner. Then note date, and names of attendees. This is your reference book, it is very valuable. You can refer back to it, at any future meeting, if there is any uncertainty about what was said.

In todays' regulatory environment, a notebook may one day defend your honour, because you will have the information of who, what, when and where meetings happened. So store your notebooks for the statute of limitations.

Competitors

No, I do not ask you to focus on them, that would be dumb. Focussing on them sends them your energy!

You should be aware of your competitors and their activity in your client. However, the more you can leave them out of your focus the better. Every time you mention their name in your clients earshot, you are advertising them! Remember the age old adage 'Bad publicity can still be good advertising!'

When running a major campaign, I often ban the competitors name being used in the organisation I lead. They have to be referred to only in oblique terms when absolutely necessary, once the qualification is done and we know we can, and will win!

You just need to keep them in your periphery vision and hearing, so you know if they do anything unexpected. Otherwise, your qualification and planning should have pretty much covered what you expect they will do. More alertness is required near the closing stages when a change in the field, or a silver bullet from a competitor could require immediate action from you. However, the competitor may never be your focus.

Your priority focus is always on winning your clients business!

Follow Up

Follow Up

Now, please do not go and get all offended here! Of course you understand you have to follow up, but are you sure you are following up everyone, and often enough?

A Sales Legend will deliver on every commitment without fail, therefore rarely having to apologise for a promise not honoured. This can be a commitment made by anyone in their own organisation, or in partnership with them, that affects their sales process.

Interestingly, I recently wrote an article on the key elements of Solution Selling. I received feedback from many top salespeople who told me they considered 'Follow-Up' the most important factor in their success. They confirmed they rarely had a competitor who did it well, and that it was a key differentiator for them.

A sales process is a project in itself. The Account Manager also needs to be a project manager and ensure everything is delivered to the client on time. Every commitment made, no matter how small must be honoured if you want to eliminate your competitors.

I have hit the head on the nail here! So few salespeople actually do this well, that this can be a killer part of your strategy in itself. You can eliminate some of your competitors by raising the bar to win so high, that only you are going to meet it.

Follow Up is a killer action. If you do it extremely well and ensure all deliverables and commitments are met 100% on time, then you are already almost unique. Your clients will be very impressed and subliminally you are influencing them that your solution represents quality, reliability and will not be one that keeps the CIO awake at night. If your clients' personal buyer motivation is being risk averse, this will be a strength in your campaign.

As the project leader for your sales campaign, you need to follow up every single person on every single commitment they made to you, your team, or your client. You even need to follow up that others on your team have followed up!

So, for example, if you are expecting the marketing department to deliver new folders for your proposal by the 23rd, then the follow up list will look something like this in your agenda:

16th Check with marketing that the printer is still on time

17th Check Marketing did follow up and get answer

22nd Ask Marketing to verify that the printing is ready and will be delivered tomorrow as expected.

23rd When folders have arrived, go to marketing and check them for quality

This is your sales campaign, so a late print delivery, or a mistake in the printing affects you, no one else has that priority and focus!

If something needs fixing, at least you will hopefully have time, because you have appropriate deadlines and follow up.

> *A major sales campaign, where I was coach for the bid team, almost resulted in a No Bid because of a small print error!*
>
> *We used to print specific title covers for inside our bid responses, these were always from the same template but the name and details of the client were on every sheet.*

> The Account Manager failed to follow up the printing, it was two days late and at the time of assembly I was doing a final Q and A, and decided to verify the client details in small print.
>
> The phone number listed was not just wrong, it was of our clients major competitor ! (You guessed – it was a previous bid)
>
> The Bid Close time was 09:00 the next morning. We had to find a solution within 18 hours. We did, but our bid arrived at 08:58 just as the security guys were on standby to open the box, after which time it would have been too late!
>
> The lack of follow up of a small detail was an act of stupidity on the part of the salesperson, and it almost cost them the chance to bid.
>
> Ten minutes of follow up at the appropriate time would have prevented this almost disaster, and saved the team having to work stupid hours to ensure assembly of the final document. The plan was previously on schedule to have the bids completed and delivered by 16:00 the day before closure!
>
> This salesperson had lost a lot of respect from a very high performance bid team, and thus they would be not so enthusiastic about doing his next bid!

So, as the person whose primary focus is winning this bid, you must follow up every single day. You need to follow up:

Internally, every person who committed to deliver anything to you, your team, or your client.

Externally, every supplier or partner, with whom you are working as part of your sales process.

The Client, ensure they have delivered to you the things they committed to deliver. This will usually be information needed, introductions, appointments and meetings, diagrams, samples or anything else involved in your sales process.

Management, you will be reliant on certain members of your management team to authorise resources, direct reports, support meetings, supply decisions etc. You must be unafraid to follow up your management team to ensure they also deliver, and on time.

Who Else? Think about others that you need to be sure have delivered, or even been advised they need to deliver, components that affect your campaign. Think of caterers, secretaries, room bookings, room equipment and preparation, reception being aware an important client is arriving, dress rules for a meeting. It may not be your job to arrange all this, but you need to follow up the person whose role it is. Make sure they can confirm each action has been completed.

I have lost count of the hours in my career that have been wasted, and clients unimpressed or de-motivated, waiting outside meeting rooms being used by someone else (and an uncomfortable discussion about who booked what and when ensues); IT have not delivered the projector, or it doesn't work with the laptop; Someone forgot to order the catering. Another frustration is waiting whilst the projector is recalibrated to each speakers' computer! All presentations should be on the one designated, already functional pc.

The salesperson tells the client it is the fault of others, but the cold, hard fact is the fault lies with only one person – the salesperson did not follow up! The other hard fact is the Client is far from enthusiastic.

Accept here and now – it is NOT acceptable for a client to witness any of this crap mentioned above! It is NOT acceptable for a client to receive a faulty piece of printing for a million dollar deal, or even a thousand dollar deal! It is your fault if the client receives anything but a smooth, warm welcome, well run meetings and flawless proposals!

Follow up all your speakers the day before a client meeting, ensure they have the right times and are ready to speak up to 15 minutes earlier if required. Ask each speaker ahead of time to always have a back up speaker, even if that is you, and to provide you a copy of their slides. Make sure everyone has your mobile number, so if the tea service persons' train is late, they can call you to ensure tea is ready! If someone wakes to find a crisis in the family, and cannot attend, they can call you!

Impress upon your speakers the need for them to be on time and ready, have their presentation preloaded on the laptop that works with the projector. Have someone, if possible, follow up and ensure each speaker is on time. People can get busy and forget the time, it is less important to them than to you. Follow Up!

I am sure you have got the message, it is your campaign, you have the focus, you need to follow up everything and everyone, every day!

Broad Spectrum Selling – *Legends Secret Number Three*

To help soften your style of follow up, and prevent being accused of harassment, here is a secret that will help boost your presence in peoples' minds.

Broad spectrum selling, is all about doing what you are exceptional at, every day with everyone! Again this is a holistic secret, one that can positively impact your whole life, as it is a habit forming secret. What I mean by broad spectrum selling is actually selling yourself,

and your clients, and your team members to everyone all the time.

Your profile can be so high that those you pass in the corridor will ask how your latest campaign, or client, is doing? People will ask ' What Can I do to help?' Remember:

ALL MANNER OF UNFORSEEN THINGS AND EVENTS WILL OCCUR TO ASSIST YOU.

Sell, sell, sell and damned well Sell!

It is what you do incredibly well, so do it. Raise your profile, make those around you feel involved and part of your success. Flood the world with your charisma, passion and success – you see everyone loves to be part of a success story. The more others support and help you, the more sales you can work on and close, the more successful you become! The more you have the support of others, the more they feel involved, the easier your day is! Tasks that support you and your projects will be higher priority for others, and your follow up will take less time and be appreciated and not seen as a harassment.

You can disguise follow up in sales chatter. For example you can give a five minute 'update' to the marketing department on your campaign, and as an aside check out how the printing project is going. You could put your head through the door of a senior manager, and give a 2 minute brief on how well it is going, gently sneaking in a reminder that he was going to contact someone who could help you.

How cool is that?

It takes the same time as basic follow up but removes any negativity and room for confrontation or offence. Probably sounds silly and far too simple, but this really is a powerful secret.

> *Recently, I worked with an Account Director, for a major channel partner. John was very adept at Broad Spectrum Selling, and he also always did around 130% of quota every quarter.*
>
> *Everyone that could affect his campaigns, in any part of this very large software company, knew what John was doing and what he was working on. They were positive about him, and words like committed, passionate, driven, successful were used to describe him.*
>
> *John did not work excessive hours but he used many of the legendary secrets and techniques that are in this guide and had enormous support from the CEO right through the organisation. If it was for John, it got priority in most departments!*

Now, I promised a holistic benefit and here it is. If you Broad Spectrum Sell to everyone around you, again you will be astonished at how much support you receive, often from unexpected sources.

> *Remember, Kamal from Secret Number Two?*
>
> *Well, he also excelled at Broad Spectrum Selling. When he would see someone he knew, he would say ' You know I am working on the new network design for Parliament now, and it is going quite well' He got all sorts of responses including direct offers of assistance.*

> *From: 'Gee, my Uncle works in IT there maybe he can help you if you need any information about the existing system'*
>
> *To: the lunch shop who offered, for the last week of the bid, to deliver team lunches each day, so that the team could keep working. This lunch bar did not even have a delivery service, so it meant they willingly sent one of their staff each day with the lunches!*

This can and will affect your personal life too. The crèche where you leave your kids may be more flexible, your family and friends will understand what you are doing, and others will offer to help you with everyday tasks.

> *I sell every day, I cannot help myself, it is part of a life habit for me.*
>
> *Now, my project is 999. My friends ask me regularly how I am going, they try to arrange events at a time when they will cause least disruption to my schedule. Several sales colleagues have sent me information on what they would love to see covered in 999, the help they seek in selling.*
>
> *Our housekeepers retired husband has offered to take over some tasks that my partner and I need to do such as order and collect some new glass panels for the house. He arrived two days ago with a beautiful purple orchid in a pot because he noticed I didn't have my usual flowers around me. I hadn't made time available to go and get them!*
>
> *Our housekeeper does all sorts of extra tasks such as baking bread and delivering it, buying the milk for us and just offering help in any way she can.*

Friends recently changed the date of a dinner party so that they would not impact my writing schedule.

Several colleagues love what we are doing so much they are already telling others, and their companies about 999. I did not ask them to, but they are caught up in our passion and commitment to success.

All of this voluntary support comes from the fact that each one of these people is helping us finish this project, because they love to be part of something that has passion, and that they believe will be a success. My daily selling keeps them informed and feeling involved. We are of course, incredibly grateful for this support.

We will explore later, in Reputation and Networking section, a powerful extension of Broad Spectrum Selling - building your own brand.

You and I have just shared a secret with unlimited personal potential!

Walking The Floor

Sales Legends are also Leaders of people. People want to be associated with luminary people, those who appear to move with their own source of energy and light.

As an extension of Broad Spectrum Selling, a salesperson can spread their warmth, charisma and passion around their own company, their clients organisation, and their partners companies. They can be seen as a luminary leader, a person to whom people are attracted and want to associate with.

Set aside some time, daily if possible, to walk around your own company (off the sales floor) and just connect briefly with people in support areas. Tell them what you are doing, use One Minute More technique, smile, radiate warmth and enthusiasm. Show you care about the people who support you in your work as a Sales Legend. You do not have to commit huge amounts of time, but say 30 minutes a day just to build on your support team.

You must be genuine in this connection, if you do not give a damn in your heart about these people, then do not expect the same results. It is simple – if you show you care, they will care too!

This is a technique of a Wolf, and there is nothing to stop you adding 'Wolf' to your reputation as a sales achiever. You will be really surprised at how much more support and energy you will receive in return, and at how many miles people will willingly walk for you .

> *Once an amazing, yet simple, winning strategy was presented to me by an office junior. He was a bit of an intellectual, and he had been thinking about how we needed to win a particular client. He was talking to his Father about strategy and got an idea that he thought might help us.*
>
> *It sure did!*

Celebrate any small wins, and steps forward, in your campaign with the people you meet. Pass on great news from another department or sales person. Good news motivates people, and after awhile, they will subliminally associate you with feeling good.

Great Leaders of organisations know how to use this technique to have a finger on the pulse of their companies.

They also understand the benefits of a highly motivated work force!

If you can embrace this small step, you are not only eliciting more support and a smoother path to winning, but you are building your reputation as a Sales Legend whilst following up any part of your campaigns in a positive way. Your work will have higher profile than other sales people who stop taking the time to do this. You will get priority on time.

When you win, share your success also broadly. Let each person you speak to, or see, feel that they somehow contributed to your success. Walking the Floor after a win is a fabulous energy booster for your next campaign, and a shot of motivation to all the people buried in the company administration and bureaucracy day after day.

People often ask me, how do I get up, and go again, after an exhausting campaign? Sharing your success is the fastest way I know to regain your energy!

These last two steps also form part of your need to motivate and lead everyone that can affect your Sale. Order processing, logistics, operations, legal, finance, accounting, warehousing, marketing and the senior management team are a crucial part of your success. If you can keep them motivated and passionate about your campaigns, you will have a lot of shoulders to stand on, and rise above the herd to win, and win again!

Project Management

Why does so much responsibility to follow up fall on your shoulders?

Winning matters to you more than anyone else, you are directly impacted by a win or a loss. It affects your income, your pride, your reputation and your motivation.

Therefore, you must be the Project Manager of your sales campaign. You must take ALL the responsibility for the win or loss. No excuses, no exceptions. This is what being a great salesperson is all about. You chose this exciting profession.

> *I had a discussion with Sara, a salesperson recently who told me she never knew it would be this hard. She chose sales because she didn't want the responsibility of management. She had not understood that she would in fact be a manager of many, so much responsibility but little real authority!*
>
> *Sara had envisaged a life in a nice suit, with nice accessories. She could imagine her life on the road in her nice car, popping in to see clients and selling them things they needed. Now she was finding that orders were delivered late, things she sold were out of stock, there were contract problems and she was missing her numbers. She believed none of this was her fault.*
>
> *Sara was somewhat shocked when I told her she was suffering from Prima Donna Syndrome, and that she had to accept total responsibility if she sold items that were out of stock (even unknowingly), or if things were delivered unexpectedly late. I asked her why she thought there were contract problems with her clients, she of course felt it was the fault of poor quality legal staff. On investigation it was of*

course her fault, Sara was agreeing to conditions with her clients that were not compatible with company policy.

She had very scant relationships with most other departments than her own. Her reputation was that of a 'spoilt brat'. She was perceived as arrogant, self focussed and lazy. She had a lot of work to do, and a career choice decision to make.

I explained to her she was like a friend of mine who joined the army to be paid whilst completing a University degree in psychology. She never expected to actually have to go to war! She had only considered the positives of the Army, she forgot the first responsibility of the army recruit was to defend her country!

I asked Sara to take a week off and consider if she had it in her to take a different approach, and accept total responsibility for all her clients, her actions and reactions, and learn some drastically different habits.

The good news is that Sara, this year, may top the sales ladder in her company. She did accept total responsibility, she made a lot of apologies and asked for another chance. Sara now tells me she does not have any of the problems that besieged her before!

As a Sales Person, you must accept total responsibility for winning or losing your campaigns.

If you cannot handle the heat, then choose to seek out a new career today!

STRATEGY

Strategy

Top achievers in selling solutions and high value capital equipment, or in maintaining long term sales relationships will know the importance of strategy.

It is the planning, thinking and prediction of which type of sales campaign will get you across the line first. It takes into consideration your position, your competitors position, the needs of your client and what actions will be necessary to win in each environment.

Now as we have said before, this is not a sales course, this is a coaching guide. I am not going to outline generic strategies and give them cute, or military names – you are not in a war, you are in a sales campaign. There are many similarities, but there are also many differences, and taking a too warlike approach to strategy can be more harmful than helpful. It is a bit 80's and a bit too masculine, and all out sweaty, for the environment we experience in the 21st millennium. So no flanking, or classic full frontals in 999!

You should have in place two strategies unless your sale is a onetime hit! There are few sales that fit this category, in most cases sales people want to build a relationship for the long term and open potential for future sales.

Client Strategy

First, you need a sound business development strategy for each client, to build your business for today, and for the rest of your career. This should be at a high level, and cover the overall approach to this client with always an objective of gaining business beyond the present known opportunity.

This is where you can reference your political map to ensure you are always building towards broad and deep coverage both vertically and horizontally in this client. You will need to consider what influences need to be applied where, and importantly for what reason. What outcomes do you see every stage of your strategic plan delivering, and when? No point in making high level connections and then wasting them, they need to be developed and nurtured when not connected to an existing deal. This is what the foundations of lifelong business relationships are made of. This also helps you avoid regulatory traps, and these become far more stringent at the time of closing large deals.

If your excellent, high level strategic relationships are a normal part of your life within your client, they form part of your network and they are public knowledge, then they are far less likely to cause any issue once a new Request for Proposals is issued.

This would normally be a proactive strategy, where most of your planning is executed without the need for rapid change. A river that moves slowly and progressively towards the sea causes little damage to the environment. As this is a planned, unhurried approach to the long term relationship, a corporate strategy rarely needs to be revisited less than every six months or so – and may last several years with only slight adjustments.

Areas that will fall into this planning will include, but are not limited to:

Ensuring your client executives and relevant staff are aware of the strengths of your company and its' people. They should be kept abreast of changes in key positions, your own companys' corporate strategy, missions and goals. They should be given annual reports and the finance and administrative executives should know each other and feel able to call. Your plan should cover who in your client will be interested in which of your companys' events. They should be regularly briefed on changes in technology and new services offered. There should be a schedule of meetings throughout the year where you have the chance to ask senior people in your client if they have projects coming up where you could participate.

You should have knowledge of your competitors who are trying to also play a long term role in your clients future. You need to have a plan in place that allows you to gather competitive intelligence on any serious and committed competitor. The guys who appear when a deal is announced, and are not seen in between, will be less of a threat if you get this strategic plan approved and supported by your team.

You should document your weaknesses as a supplier to this client, and within the competitive landscape. You, and your team, should be always cognisant of any opportunity that presents itself to strengthen any perceived weakness at any opportunity, even on the fly! I always recommend knowing your weaknesses far better than your strengths. Your competitors will know your strengths, because every company on the planet has a PR team that boasts loudly of strength. Your competitors however, may not know all your weaknesses, but those they do know about they will actively use against you. In your strategic plan, there should be cover for every known weakness you have. How will you satisfy this client regardless of those weaknesses?

Ideally, you should have some plans about how to unbalance, or undermine, your competitors position over a period of time. Destabilisation of a competitor, without being obvious, is also a powerful long term strategic weapon.

Included in your strategic plan should be some review periods where you can measure the performance of yourself and your team against significant milestones. I have seen too many eloquently worded, long term strategic plans, that have absolutely no measurability, accountability or in the end effectiveness. They begin to gather dust in a pile somewhere of beautiful but useless strategic plans, written at great cost that yielded no return on investment.

Write your plan in a simple way, that everyone can understand without falling asleep or suffering distraction from boredom. Forget fancy diagrams, and pretty graphs, and piles of useless facts that do not help anyone.

I have seen paralysis by analysis rife in the production of beautiful strategic documents that actually say bugger all really! Poor quality strategic plans are a criminal waste of human resource, ink and trees!

Do not spend time proving your spreadsheet expertise, by producing pivot tables of every conceivable cut of the previous periods' business. All that will really matter in the end, is did you – or did you not – grow the top and bottom line results from this client to meet, or exceed, expectations? That as a highly paid, top achiever is the expected outcome of your job.

That, therefore, is the sole purpose of this planning document. Does it answer the following questions?

Will you get at least the desired result from this client? How?

Have you maximised your opportunity within this client?

If your answers are yes, then you have made a sound strategic plan.

It is that simple.

Campaign Strategy

So you have an opportunity to win, a strategic plan in place to build the relationship within your client, how the hell are you going to win it?

That is the core question we have to consider when planning a campaign strategy. First you qualified your opportunity and came to the conclusion that you could, and would, win. Now, in that qualification process you will have given some thought as to what was necessary for you to win, and you believed you had access to all those people and things. They form the basis of your campaign strategy.

When considering competitors, you must focus only on the most important ones, and not become distracted by a competitor who will never win. Ask yourself, if I do not win this deal, who will? Who has the potential to outsell me? These are the people you need to understand and have plans in place to manage.

This should not be a long document, and if you have the first client strategic plan in place then you need only focus this plan on the deal at hand.

The biggest question is always

What value can I offer?

What will give your client an advantage, hopefully a competitive advantage, over a solution from one of your competitors? Can you translate this into a business benefit/s for your client?

Remember, your client will not be interested that your solution has more bells and whistles if they do not need them. In fact, it may even be considered a negative.

> Some years back we needed to buy a substantial colour printer for the sales office. We needed good colour, fast speed, reliability, easy to clear jams and reasonably priced inks. Apart from basic printer features, that was all we needed.
>
> We had an idea we would like a particular printer commonly used in advertising agencies. One of our suppliers had one, and they raved about it. So we called the sales person.
>
> He came to see our office manager, she felt the price offered was good and referred him to me for a quick approval.
>
> Well, Craig the sales person decided to start selling me the bells and whistles as soon as he got through my door. He convinced me the printer had many features, actually features I began to realise we would never use. I began to wonder, amongst the noise, if we could get a similar printer with less features at a better price. I thought maybe they have a competitor with an older model, but has the basic functions we need at a good price.
>
> So, Craig left without the order he expected. Canon had a printer that met our needs, without so many features and we saved a few hundred dollars.
>
> Craig chose the wrong strategy, he should have taken a minimal approach and probably would have left with an order!

Your client will really only care about things that matter to him or her, and the business needs. If you have an added feature that you believe is important to mention, then ensure it offers your clients business a benefit they can sell to someone (internally or externally). It may be that, with your product, an additional service could be offered to their clients, this can be a winner! Or it saves productivity time, still possibly a winner if they have resourcing issues. Selling a 'hot' feature that your client has no need for, may cause them to consider things like operational simplicity, or price, or value for money!

So ensure your campaign plan plays right into the hands of solving their business needs, and providing for expansion if that was required. Ensure your plan covers off a briefing, of the excellent match of your technology to their business needs, to all who are involved or influencing the decision. Remember, if the solution is a new phone system the receptionist will likely be at least an influencer, do not over look important people like the users and their potential impact.

> *We were once convinced we had an outstanding solution for a banking environment. However, our competitors also met the basic requirements and looked good in the test environment. They were also cheaper, as the technology was older.*
>
> *We knew we had two competitive advantages that could not be seen:*
>
> - *load capability – we could handle more concurrent sessions than our competitor*
>
> - *interface – we had a very user friendly interface, but to a very experienced user (such as in the test environment) was not obvious.*

So we suggested to the bank that we set up a live demo, via the web, and that the bank invite a control group of customers to trial the solutions. We agreed this was not a cheap idea, but what a fabulous way for a bank that had a by-line '.....we exceed our customers expectations' to delight their users!

The Bank loved the idea, and one week into the control test, we had almost 100% of the customer preferences! The reliability test for load, where several thousand customers were rewarded to log in almost simultaneously, was a shoe in for us.

Our campaign strategy was a lot about how to demonstrate two end user visible benefits that improved our customers' commitment to service excellence.

Flexibility and Speed

When writing a campaign strategy, look for all the traps that competitors will lay, and lay an alternate trap in advance of therm.

A trap is a space that a salesperson will likely fall into, forced to expose a weakness. This must be done with finesse and subtlety or it will not work. Traps are often laid by your team such as consultants, presales engineers, or senior management.

Alternate traps, are laid when you suspect your competitor will lay a trap for you. Thus, if they spring their trap, you have already rendered it useless.

For example:

> You know your competitor is likely to mention to your client, that your company just lost a significant customer in the same industry as your customer. Your alternate trap could be to front this one directly with '
>
> "You will no doubt hear that our company just lost Acme Chemicals as a customer. I wanted to reassure you about this event.
>
> Acme, as you know has been implementing some cost cutting initiatives and unfortunately despite our excellent relationship there for many years, the buyer had no choice but to opt for a less expensive solution, with loss of a few benefits for their customers.
>
> For example the lower cost system will no longer automatically schedule logistics, so customers will have to wait a little longer for delivery. As we agreed earlier, your company holds logistics as a high priority, so I do not believe this should impact our business relationship.
>
> Additionally there is an added benefit for you, we will have some additional very experienced chemical industry staff ready to accelerate the roll out your project, if we win."

Now, if your competitor decides to spring this trap in your client, they will be ineffective. Your client already has an answer and your competitor looks in poor form for having raised it. Your client will likely defend your position, even using your words.

Trapping requires good campaign strategy, perfect timing and great sensitivity. It is very powerful and can produce a winning element in your campaign. Be aware though – everything in your trap, or any alternate trap, must be 100% true otherwise it will badly backfire. If you have no answer for an impending trap, you only have two choices:

1. Decide to wing it, hoping your client will not find out.

2. Confess the truth, and offer a sound proposition why it will not affect your client.

Trapping is also a proactive strategy, but in some areas where you are unsure how your competitor will behave, or whether your client will see a weakness, you will need to have reactive strategies ready for fast deployment.

Ask yourself, or ideally your team to do this for you, what traps they could see that may possibly be sprung. What could go wrong, and if it does is it covered in your plan?

Now, you should have also planned your campaign to include traps that you will lay for your competitor. Use their weaknesses against them. Often the importance of a strength, or weakness to a client will be pre-empted by his or her perception of the particular event and possible impact.

In a sales campaign for a large Telco switching solution, we were bidding a best in class solution for a multi vendor environment. Now it is difficult to explain here, so let me try and give a bid scenario. We were bidding two interoperable equipment brands Acme Switches and Jones Hubs. The two companies had worked together on joint development and their solutions worked seamlessly in high tech environments with a high degree of reliability. There were a perfect solution, and we knew we could and would win.

Our key competitor was bidding a sole brand solution from Williams, however it had some inherent weaknesses in such difficult environments.

Four days before the final decision was to be made, I was awakened very early in the morning with a phone call from the USA telling me that Williams had just announced a purchase of Jones. This meant that our competitor could now be perceived as having an advantage.

Our reactive strategy was simple. Whoever got to the client first with this unsettling news was going to win, because each person would convince the client of advantage. We planned to be first, we knew the key decision maker well and we had a consultant on site who was a trusted adviser.

We got our consultant out of bed early and asked him to go in and 'ambush' the decision maker at the door. We briefed him as follows:

Tell Jim we have great news. Jones has just been bought by Williams, which means it will have significant funding put into R and D moving forward.

A sound investment for the Telco. The good news is this announcement does not affect our ability to deliver a world class solution next week, and of course Acme (the main component and project lead) will be unaffected by the usual corporate chaos and nervousness of employees that follows a buy like this! We could not get you any information about *whether Williams will discontinue their existing hub line, that is something you need to check with them, as it could be a short term investment if they stop supporting this line, in lieu of releasing new technology from the Jones investment.*

Jeff, our consultant did this. He got to the decision maker first. He overheard, a few minutes later, that the competitor rang Jim.

Jim was overheard 'Yes, I heard they bought Jones. Not necessarily an advantage. The Jones hubs will not be immediately operable, so that will delay the project. Can you guarantee me that the current Williams hubs will now be supported for the five year life of this solution?'

The need for speed, this reactive strategy had worked. Had the competitor got to Jim first, with a different spin on the news, our likely feedback would have been ' Now Jones hubs can be included in the deal and we can have an equivalent solution for a lower price!' We would have been under price pressure, and they would have had an advantage instead of us.

We won!

Although this was something completely unexpected, we had rapid plans in place. We had prepared these for back up of other possible information, that may highlight any weakness, reaching our client. The fact that Jeff, our consultant was in place at the time, was also not a coincidence but a carefully executed part of our campaign plan. We needed someone trusted on site in the event of any unexpected activity. Jeff was not directly working on this project, he was assisting in the design of a new go to market, customer premises solution. His presence was therefore not a breach of governance, but he was there if and when we needed him!

We were able to just deploy an existing, back up, plan B for this unexpected situation.

Campaign strategy is all about flexibility, speed, and meeting the customers' needs every step of the way.

Art of Distraction and Misinformation

When you have a formidable competitor, you may need specific types of strategy to weaken their game.

Enter the Art of Distraction and Misinformation.

This can be an intelligent and unpredictable (for competitors) part of your campaign plan, however it must be executed with care and precision.

It is perfectly possibly to build into your campaign plans actions that will distract your competitor at key strategic times. This would normally be some kind of red herring, that on the surface appears outrageous and could appear to affect your campaign, yet actually you have already settled it with your client. An example could be something like the departure of your CEO, but provided this has been fully put to bed with your client and they are relaxed about it, then it could be used to distract. You could whisper in certain places that you know are not in confidence, that everyone on your team is concerned that such an event may impact your business. Your competitor, if not a 999er, will likely grab this snippet and try to blow it up. It will distract them from their purpose.

Provided you do not deliberately lie, or spread malicious information, this distraction technique is very useful. Stay within your integrity and have this all planned in your strategy so it does not become loose cannon balls.

I have thrown a red herring like the possibility of a revised network redesign at the technical level to distract from a meeting at the C level where some business changes or value add services were discussed. My competitors salesperson was so busy worrying about the new design, that he had no knowledge of the meeting and was caught out on the value base at a later stage. I did not lie, we did review our design, and found it to be correct still.

Misinformation can be carefully used if you happen to meet staff from your key competitor at an event, or in the street. If they ask you 'How is your Acme deal going?' It is perfectly within a planned approach, to have some comments ready. You can distract with misinformation, that is not malicious, such as ' I hear you guys are doing a fabulous job in there, makes it tough for us!' If your whole team can say the same when they meet competitor staff, the story will be reinforced! You know, it must be true as it comes from several sources.

What you said was actually true, and pretty meaningless, but your competitor is hoping to find an Achilles heel, so will likely jump on it. This may cause your competitor to ease off the pressure as they feel you believe they are winning.

Remember, when you were a kid and a story got passed around how wrong and exaggerated it became as it went from ear to ear? Well, a comment like that on the street can be translated back, and by the time it reaches the salesperson, it will likely be repeated as 'They said that they are losing the deal to us, they have given up!'

Giving your competitors assurance that they are running a clever and fabulous campaign, congratulating them on any small win along the way, is a great way to keep them distracted and less focussed on beating you. You can also encourage your competitors to brag about their own campaign, and this can be very enlightening! Bragging is trap that a 999er must never fall into though – humility is good at this time, your focus is winning, not your ego – time for that after you win!

If you can weave some appropriate distractions through your campaign plan, then you will have some fun without losing focus, and know your competitors are chasing their tails, whilst you flawlessly execute the rest of your campaign.

The Art of Distraction, is just that - an art, it must be used to create masterpieces of strategic planning and not predictable bulk canvasses.

The Field Change – *Legends Secret Number Four*

This is a tactic that you can include in your planning. It is often a deal winner, but carries a degree of risk if executed poorly.

At a later point in your campaign, it is possible, to introduce a positive factor that can change the playing field. This means changing the basis of your bid by adding more value. It could be you bid a solution containing version 1.0 of software, and now 2.0 is available and you offer to include an upgrade that version. It is more effective however, if you can introduce a new element altogether.

It may be that you can offer to implement your solution in a phased way that minimises risk, but this would be difficult for your competitor to do. It may be that you offer a customised piece of software for your client that would give them huge business advantage as an add on after your solution is implemented. It could be that you can reconstruct your offer in a much more effective way for financing. It could be that you offer an alternative that is different than asked for in say an RFP or tender document, but offers considerable client advantage.

This means your key competitors have to respond very quickly to catch up and match your value. If you are a smaller company, competing against a bureaucratic giant, then it may be that your competitor cannot respond in time.

It may be that you can use your competitors lack of flexibility, complexity of decision making, or arrogance against them. However, you must do this at a crucial time in your campaign that allows your client time to consider the change, yet gives your competitor minimum response time.

This is kind of like changing the rules of a football game, in the last five minutes when the score is even. One team is aware of the changed rules, and the other team has to find out in play. Changing the shape of the playing field is a powerful weapon, that if executed extremely well with precision timing, can win you a deal.

> *Working for a niche player in global services, this was often a tactic deployed to stop a large competitor in their tracks.*
>
> *After I left this company, my key competitor headhunted me*

> *with the open admission that they had never been able to beat our team! Not once in 3 years!*
>
> *We used their inability to swiftly respond to any change, and slow decision process, to defeat them time and time again. Interestingly, their strategy was always predictable. Born of arrogance, they chose a classic, old world full frontal attack. When challenged by our company, they simply resorted to blatant ridicule, and lost integrity. They laid lots of traps, but we had anticipated them because they were fairly rusty!*

The Field Change is very effective, and incredibly satisfying. It is an intelligent, and not well understood tactic for winning complex deals. It can often be executed at several levels above you, if the senior relationships are in place, and that is also very effective. Especially if it contains a strong business benefit, it will help to execute a two part tactic simultaneously at the business unit or C level and the buyer level. At the same time as the business unit is asking for the new feature, the buying office has the answer! Pretty much a done deal!

One important note to remember, you first must submit a compliant document, before trying to change the field, else you will confuse your buyer and may lose. If you deploy this tactic too early, your competitor may be able to roll right over the top of you, and capitalise on your idea.

The Gold Bullet – *Legends Secret Number Five*

Bullets are powerful advantages that you can offer if and when required to win.

There are two kinds:

> Silver – These are smaller and can be used along the way when required. However, they are likely to be advantages that your competitor can also match when pushed.

> Gold – These are almost unbeatable winners, act like magic, and we are ecstatic if we can find them for any opportunity. They are the killer shot!

We will focus here on Gold Bullets as once you understand them, you will understand silver bullets.

Gold Bullets are kept for the final master stroke. They are made from an advantage you hold, but did not reveal earlier in the campaign. Sometimes we do not have them until the 11th hour, but we must recognise them immediately and have them ready to fire.

Gold Bullets will execute your competitors campaign!

We have referred a couple of times, earlier in the document, to a golden bullet. Under integrity, we explained the example of the senior decision maker who accepted the ride in the corporate jet – a clear golden bullet and an opportunity to close the deal. The second example, was under the section Arrogance, and was the National Director who revealed his lack of empathy for the large airport deal. Another example, was in Corporate Governance, where we used a combination of Change the Field, and a Gold Bullet to win a deal before the Tender was even distributed!

It is a formidable combination of tactical deployment in a strong strategic campaign plan.

A Gold Bullet is often not revealed early, and is frequently handed to you by your competitors' actions. You have to be alert enough to see it instantly and respond accordingly. It may not even be obvious to your client, it doesn't have to be.

A Gold Bullet can also be handed to you unknowingly by a client. Perhaps they inadvertently reveal something that triggers in your mind an advantage you can offer that will ignite the deal, but you had not realised was important before.

A Gold Bullet can be a piece of information, that you know right from the beginning is in your arsenal, yet you will not deploy it until necessary or appropriate. For example, you may know of a new feature and benefit coming in a new release that is highly confidential, however your current proposal is already strong, so you can hold this benefit back until the last minute and only deploy if needed.

A Gold Bullet is a piece of information, or a benefit, that you recognise represents your winning strike. It is an irrefutable or unbeatable shot!

Many large complex opportunities have a golden bullet, if you do not know what it is, then be alert for it when it shows itself. It is kind of like the skull in PC games that one has to find, to reveal the code to move to the next level!

In every campaign, look for silver bullets, the smaller lesser events that can be deployed to accelerate your campaign and put pressure on competitors. Keep yourself very alert for the Gold Bullet that hands you the win!

I have been part of many campaigns where the competitor had access to a Gold Bullet, but fortunately for me, did not deploy it.

> "I HAVE SEEN PARALYSIS BY ANALYSIS RIFE IN THE PRODUCTION OF BEAUTIFUL STRATEGIC DOCUMENTS THAT ACTUALLY SAY BUGGER ALL REALLY!
>
> POOR STRATEGIC PLANS ARE A CRIMINAL WASTE OF HUMAN RESOURCE, INK AND TREES!"

THE CONSORTIUM

The Consortium

Sales Legends display an extraordinary talent for assembling winning consortiums, when required, to win a large opportunity. They demonstrate leadership in this environment, and excel in conflict resolution, thus creating an environment of win/win solutions being proposed to clients.

A Consortium should be defined as a group of entities, usually companies, who collaborate on a single proposal or client to provide a complex solution ordinarily not possible to offer alone. They are frequently seen in large outsourcing and communications bids, and in geographical environments like the EU, but can be used in every industry where a complex solution is needed. They are also seen in markets like Real Estate, although usually on a smaller scale.

The head bidder, may or may not be you. The person who pulls together the consortium, may or may not be you. A Sales Legend can work within a consortium arranged by a third party, or take steps to create one whether or not they will lead the bid.

The lead, or head bidder is usually selected for a one of the following reasons:

- Funding – they will be an organisation of substance, able to fund such a bid, and the financing of the total solution. The billing may be split, or unified, depending on the solution and the client preference.

- They are the Project Managers and prefer to manage the whole process including bidding and billing.

- They will be submitting the highest value, or majority part, of the solution. Let's face it, no sense comes of a company who bids 5% of the solution (albeit an essential and critical piece) would be the head or lead, it will make no sense to your client.

- They have an excellent, high value strategic relationship with the client.

- Perhaps they are the only consortium members who will front the bid, or the outsourcers, or a large telecommunications provider or industrial contractor.

All good reasons, and why, at the beginning stages of forming a Consortium, a meeting needs to be held to establish the distribution of responsibility and accountability. A 'good neighbours' policy document, not too detailed, should be provided and signed by all parties agreeing to the roles assigned.

The lead bid needs to also provide contract information early so that all cooperative suppliers can be sure they can meet the requirements that will form the main contract. If this is not done, I am sure you can guess what happens later, even after the sale is won it halts project implementation and revenue generation until resolved. You need to avoid this with early rational planning.

Even if you did not put together the consortium, but were either invited to join or muscled your way in, then you can still be perceived to take a leadership position. Now you have two customers, you have the consortium and your client. In both cases you need to deploy your qualification (are you in the right consortium?), focus, follow up and certainly several of your Legends secrets. From a side position, you can still be leading the others to produce a proposal worthy of your participation.

Often, we have no choice, a tender is positioned in a way that our only way to bid is via a Consortium. We would of course have known this beforehand, unless we are a very minor player. Non-compliant bids are ranked very low in client priority, especially if they only fulfil part of the solution.

No matter how big and important you are in your own industry, and lunch box, you are very unlikely to win a part solution with a solo non-compliant bid. I have seen many senior people make the mistake of not believing this.

> *I worked for a large company, who was a giant in their own industry. When it came to a Greenfield bid within a very large telecommunications company, our sales people wanted to do a partial bid.*
>
> *My counsel was simple. Does the CEO of this Telco play golf with the CEO of our company? No, but he does play with the CEO of our partner. Does the CFO of this Telco meet regularly with our CFO? No, but he does have a monthly meeting with our partner who already has a large outsourcing contract there. Do we really know any of the decision makers but one? No! Do we have a strong relationship with him? No!*
>
> *Bid as a Consortium, or not at all, else you waste time and resource that could be better deployed to a campaign you can win!*

Consortiums are incredibly important part of gaining additional business without having to do all the work, and build all the relationships. Often being part of a consortium also introduces additional new opportunity through Consortium partners, or by meeting people to whose doors you would not have had access alone.

Sometimes a supplier can be in all the shortlisted consortiums, an undefeatable position!

When considering which consortium partners to choose, or which existing consortium to join, we need to go through a hard line qualification process. We need to identify where the winning strengths will be, and if possible bring them together. If you cannot do this, and you have to join a lesser consortium, then qualify your chances of success before committing resources.

I highly recommend a course in conflict resolution for all senior salespeople, it will be of enormous help to you, not just as part of a consortium but also in your own teams under stress. These courses teach you how to get around the ego and political issues, get everyone on the same raft and rowing in the same direction! Conflict resolution skills are a rarity in good sales people, so will differentiate you, and really help you every day.

When working within a consortium, you will need to execute every action required of you within timeframes set, or it throws out a whole chain of events. Treat the consortium as you would a customer. You need to be sure that your part of the solution demonstrates extraordinary value to the client both singly, and as the sum of the parts.

If you are leading a consortium, if possible appoint a project manager to either lead for you (or be beside you). You will need to be on your best behaviour, and have skills like respect, humility, leadership qualities, follow up and the human connection as an unconscious part of your life. You need to convince everyone they can and will win if they perform well. You are the energy source who keeps everyone highly motivated and focussed on winning.

You need sound, agreed strategy. You better be sure this is a bid you can win, and the value is worth the time. It usually is!

Closing the consortium deal is difficult, especially if you do not hold the lead. It is indirect. You can still supply bullets if you have them, depending on your lead bid partner you may be able to deploy field change, but your options are limited to the areas of influence that are under your control. You must be careful that you do not, through impatience, take action that will piss off your partners or worse lose you the deal. This is where your leadership skills, and Legend Secrets, will help you help your partner close the deal.

Keep open communication with the lead, at all times, discuss every action before taking it. Reactively, in a timely manner, brief them of anything that happened at a meeting, or chance encounter, at which they were not present. The better you work with them, the easier they can close the deal. Ideally, set up an email alias for all members to communicate daily updates.

In a Consortium, communication and the human connection is critical. A Sales Legend moves wolf-like through this environment, motivating and listening to every sound, manipulating and massaging when required to achieve harmony and ultimately success.

Customer Enthusiasm

Customer Enthusiasm

The customers of a Sales legend will be very enthusiastic about them, and the solutions they provide, the value they add. Their customers will consider them trusted advisers. Their customers will go out of their way to help the Sales Legend win again and again.

The Sales Legend will achieve this through habitual use of outstanding communication techniques like the human connection, one minute more and integrity. They will build strong relationships across their clients' matrix through their focus on business needs and their ability to follow up and deliver consistently. They operate from a platform of respect, appreciation and availability.

> *I resigned from a senior sales position in a large networking vendor to take up a new role, that still could not be publicly disclosed. I sent an email to many of my clients and I particularly remember one response as a cameo moment in my career.*
>
> *My customer responded, 'Good people are rare, please call me as soon as you start your new role, maybe we can still do some business'*
>
> *In humour, I responded that perhaps I was going to a life change role, and would now be selling ladies lingerie. My customer replied in vein ' No problem, I have a wife and two daughters. Contact Me!'*

This is just a tiny example of the effect of customer enthusiasm. It almost does not matter what you are selling, if you help your customers do their job, and they enjoy working with you, then you have a customer for life!

Let us now explore some elements of what generates Customer Enthusiasm. Whilst we look at several things, each one of these has only minimal impact in isolation, they are meant to be used as collective habits to generate a high level of loyalty, and commitment, from your customer that contributes to your personal success.

How cool is it, when you see a key decision maker in a large corporation talking to your CEO at a function, and you can relax and smile knowing your name is represented 'in lights'?

It is very C-O-O-L! ☺

With some of these elements, you may be getting frustrated again and we are potentially back to egg sucking! Just stay in integrity, and ask yourself how many of these things you are consistently doing really well.

You have the eye control, it is your coaching guide, you can skip something that is irrelevant, or you do not want to read!

Selling Value Not Price

We have touched on this before, but now we are going to look at the relevance of selling value to a buyer.

It is normally only either a low performance buyer, or a buyer in an environment bound by accepting the cheapest quote, that may not appreciate a value sell. Now if you are in a position to win quickly on price, then that is a no brainer, otherwise these buyers need to be managed with caution.

Selling value is instrumental in gaining the respect of your client. If you can qualify their business needs, and demonstrate a solution that meets these needs at a fair price, then you have a fair chance of winning.

To take your sales campaign to the next level, you need to be able to not only demonstrate that you meet the needs as specified, but research the business units and try to understand where they want to go in the future. You may be in a position to offer more value add for the same money, such as scalability of solution, next generation services or contribute a business idea that enhances the existing product.

If you show that you are willing to add value to *their* business, not just your deal, this will not only delight your customers but set you apart from most salespeople. If you have good networking and human connections, then it can even be very simple acts of random assistance, for which you perceive no direct reward.

> *Leon, a colleague, was selling a piece of commercial real estate to a client who was complaining that he needed an urgent print job and that his printer had let him down. Leon knew a good printer, with a flexible production process. He had a good relationship with him through his sons' school,. Leon made the introduction and was able to solve his clients distracting print problem.*
>
> *That generated a lot of customer enthusiasm, and the client became more open with Leon about what needed to be resolved for the Real Estate transaction to move forward. Leon closed the deal two weeks earlier than anticipated.*

Selling value can take many forms, but it should always be paramount in the mind of a good sales person. In my career, I have rarely had to offer exceptional discount, because I have always sold value instead of price. I have never been too concerned about a competitor having a lower price, they usually did. My campaign profitability was almost always highest in the team.

When a client asks me for a discount, I always ask why he or she want a discount. The answers can give you valuable insight about adding value. If what they are asking is not reasonable, then sometimes I have asked what benefit they would prefer not to have in the solution, so I can offer the discount. Alternately, I am may find a way to sell a relevant added value instead of discount.

If it is the purchasing officer, after the decision is awarded, I will already know this will be the case and will have retained something of value, or a few points of margin, to satisfy the purchasing office. Sometimes, a purchasing office is responsible for day to day buying decisions, and they are rewarded based on percentages saved, thus this is an important consideration in my overall value statement.

Selling value with your solution, means you must be able to articulate and demonstrate to your client, that by buying your solution they are receiving the maximum value at a fair price.

Selling value as a person means random acts of kindness, within appropriate guidelines, and accessing a broad network at your disposal to solve problems or to offer support, or advice.

Selling value, and building this trusted relationship, may sometimes take some bizarre angles.

In a government bid, we knew our decision maker had a passion for ballet. Our company sponsored ballet and shortly a famous ballet dancer was coming to a venue nearby, and clients were invited to a VIP event.

However, as we were in a bid process with this client, we could not risk breaking the rules of governance and include her in the invitations at our cost.

We decided on a special tactic.

We explained the situation to her, and her disappointment was obvious. However, we suggested she check with her Minister if she may accept the invitation, and join the group, but pay for her own ticket and consumables. She was granted permission to do this, as no benefit was taken in kind, no advantage given. She was very enthusiastic about her chance to see this dance, and in the company of her peers.

The competitor heard about her attending, and made the wrong assumption, they lodged a complaint, triggered an investigation. You can imagine how that made the decision maker enthusiastic for their solution – not!

The investigation proved fruitless, as we had broken no regulations. We had a double whammy here – Customer enthusiasm and a trap to weaken our competitor .

Continually, look for ways to add value to your clients' business, your solution, your relationship and the sales process.

Exceeding Your Commitments

Meeting your promises, deliverables and commitments is a must in any sales process if you want to be in front. Exceeding your commitments is a way to delight, and often positively surprise, your customer. Nothing generates enthusiasm faster than someone who exceeds expectations and delivers more!

It starts with habit forming small things, if you commit to being on time, be a few minutes early (but do not camp out in reception 30 minutes before the time). If you promised donuts for morning tea, deliver special donuts that you know that are each persons' favourite. If you promised the receptionist you would bring the name of a great DVD, perhaps instead you could lend her your copy, it may not be appropriate to give her one.

It can extend to exceeding your commitments in the solution review, perhaps you can bring an additional person with you that can value add. So instead, of just communicating with you, they have also an expert in a field of relevance. Make sure of course you call in advance for meeting security and protocol requirements.

If you committed they could have access to an engineer for 2 hours, perhaps when he arrives he can casually advise that you arranged a bit of extra time for him!

If you promised some information by Tuesday, but on Monday it is ready, will it please your customer to have it one day earlier?

I could go on for pages of ideas, but I am sure you get it. If you commit something, whenever possible deliver something plus! A word of caution do not go over the top every time, or you may look a bit weird, and you will have set too high expectations. The element of surprise is powerful and delightful. Choose the most significant moments to exceed your promises for maximum effect!

How often do you meet your commitments, 100% of the time in a sales campaign? How often do you remember to plan in things that will exceed your commitments?

Understanding The Client Business

The more you can walk in the shoes of your customer, the more enthusiasm you will generate.

If the customer is large enough, and important enough to your sales result, then you should really dedicate some time to understanding their business environment and processes. Understand their success metrics and what they get excited and passionate about. Know who their competitors are, and what advantage they offer, or strive to offer.

If it is relationship based selling, in other words a more strategic long term customer, then it is worthwhile even going as far as arranging visits and briefings at some of their core business units, and even at the factory floor. It is a compliment that you wish to understand their business to be able to serve them better. You will, of course, need to have earnt some trust before taking this step.

The more you can walk in the shoes of your customers daily business, the better you will be able to understand their hot buttons and buying motivations. You will be able to be proactive in suggesting where your company could play an increased role in helping them go to market faster, better or more cost effectively.

Let us look again at that store where you buy your suits.

Imagine that the salesperson there shows that they really

need to understand your lifestyle to better advise on suit fabrics and cuts. I am yet to experience someone who cares enough, has this knowledge and wants to sell enough to do this!

They could ascertain: Do I drive myself to appointments, take a taxi or stand in a commuter train? Do I do my own laundry, and do I mind hand washing? Do I prefer to dry clean or wash? Am I allergic to , or irritated by, any fabrics or textures? How often do I need to convert the days' business suit quickly into an evening suit? Do I have colour preferences? Do I have pet likes or dislikes? What sort of image do I want to convey? Do I regularly leave my jacket on through a meeting? Is brand important to me?

If that suit salesperson could walk a day in my shoes then they could understand what fabrics, cuts and styles will work best to fit my lifestyle! They would probably engender not only customer enthusiasm, but undying lifetime loyalty and a lot of referrals!

Spend time really understanding your customers business and connecting in the language of their industry, actually being fully cognisant what that language means.

If you are considered an industry insider, that you really understand their business, their way of communicating, then it is possible you can also add value to building their business case.

Assisting the customer to build their business case is a very powerful position to be in. You can even sometimes lock out a competitor, or at least disadvantage them, at this time. You have advance notice of any customisation necessary in your solution to be the perfect fit.

You will not just be aware, but be sure, of the funding position and the reason for the project. You will also likely have confirmation of timelines, sense of urgency, budget, and buying criteria. You will have the chance to build human connections with the senior people in that business unit and possibly other support people. It is one of the most powerful positions, in which to find yourself, during the sales process.

Maximising The Matrix

Some colleagues of mine, have in certain circumstances, even had a desk allocated to them within the client company. This is most common in channel partnerships, where the sales person supporting a large value channel partner spends one, or several days a week at the office of the partner. In some instances, this has increased partnership revenue by up to 50%. However, this only works effectively if you have one partner, or at least non-competing partners, as clients.

Once you have established a trusted relationship with your client, it is possible to start developing additional relationships with many people within that organisation, and at all levels. It is even possible, for very senior sales people, considered trusted advisers and operating at the strategic level, to have open access to the senior management including the C level. These type of sales relationships are hard to beat.

If you are up against one competitively, I suggest you agree with your company a long term, strategic development plan with measurable milestones to better establish both you and your company. It will unlikely be possible for you to feel confident about winning large pieces of business, if competing with an established Trusted Adviser.

You can win, but it will take long term strategy, or an unbeatable product at an exceptional price, I have seen discounts like 80 or 90% win just because the client says it is almost free – so too good to be refused. However, rarely do the architects of those kind of deals go on to be a Trusted Adviser, and win consistently. Every individual deal has to be won, and on price! They have no other cards to deal with. Often, even the associated services still go to a trusted supplier; so there is minimal chance to improve on profitability of the total package.

This is ok strategy, if your company just wants market share at any price, but those days have kind of disappeared in the volatile economic environment of the last few decades. Fewer companies can afford this type of dealing for market share; fewer investors are excited by companies that have great market share accompanied by a bleeding bottom line.

Maximise your matrix and cover the client organisation with tier selling technique. This means you actively introduce a peering matrix of colleagues between your company and the client company. Tis will also enhance your political mapping, and provide that broad coverage you need.

Your main contact, and coach, will not feel threatened if you regularly suggest new peer connections such as your engineering team and theirs, your VP of Finance and theirs, your strategist and their CIO. These connections will need to be led as a team by you, and you will want to ensure you introduce people from your organisation you can trust and follow up. They need to understand your strategy and be kept fully briefed.

Depending on the timeline of opportunities closing, you should meet with your matrix team monthly or weekly for team briefings. This is an incredibly powerful way to quickly build your influence in an organisation, but remember these people are your responsibility and you need to be able to lead this team in a coordinated and engaging way. If appropriate, and you can engage very senior people like the two CEOs, or Board Members, you are beginning to really have a trusted and fruitful environment in which to sell.

Do not try to operate at this level, if your business is non strategic to the clients business. This is a classic mistake many large companies sales people make. To you and your company, the client is vital but to the client you are just a small part of a big solution and not seen as managing, or owning, the overall situation.

It maybe that your client relies on an outsourcer to recommend and implement anything, and the only way you will ever become strategic is if that outsourcer positions you that way. So, I guess that is an indicator of what matrix you need to develop first!

Many salespeople do not fully comprehend the human connection significance of a partner, sometimes without the embedded partner you will not win anything in that client. You are just not seen as strategic. You can change this by being strategic to your partner!

Listening Actively

We touched on this skill earlier when discussing the power of the Human Connection. We are now going to pay some more attention to this, how to achieve it and make it a habit.

Nothing is more off putting than to be interrupted, unless it is to add enthusiasm to your story. Interruptions are rude, and often mean that the person is not paying attention to the speaker. You will probably be embarrassed at how often we all do it!

It is bad enough with friends and family, but to interrupt clients is a disaster. Spend some time taking note how many times you are interrupted when speaking, or that you interrupt others. Some people rarely interrupt, if this is you that is great, but now ask yourself are you actually listening? How engaged are you with the speaker?

When your customer is speaking, it is best to hear the whole proposition, or content, before speaking yourself. You can nod, smile and use other inaudible gestures to indicate you are listening. I use eye movement, probably because I am visual I find this easiest. The more your customer speaks the better, and the more actively you can listen will set you ahead of the game. You see, most of your colleagues do not listen actively, they listen passively and their minds wander easily. They often miss something small but it may be quite relevant or important.

> *I have seen a salesperson miss a strong buying signal. It was subtle, but closable. She kept talking, and in the end she oversold her solution, and lost the deal!*
>
> *Kate is a real estate agent, and her company was using me as a coach. She specialised in very high value homes and estates. She was showing some properties to a young man and nothing so far had lit any fire in him. Then we got to a property that was right. She was busy talking, and as he made comments, Kate kept saying ' Yes, but look at this, look at that etc.' Her buyer was looking very thoughtful and then*

said, 'I like this place, I would love to look at this view every morning"

Instead of trying to close the sale there and then, Kate missed the significance of his statement, I did not feel that she even heard it, as she was already thinking about the next house on the list. She had a plan and no buyer was going to distract her!

Kate took him round several more houses, in which he showed no interest, until he said he was tired and had enough. Kate drove him back to her office, thanked him for his time, and said she would call him when she had a new listing.

She did not remember his statement in that dining room, when I asked her why she did not close. She dismissed it as insignificant, and said she felt he wasn't really ready to buy yet. Kate was upset with me that I considered she did not listen, even though I could tell her things about her clients' preferences she did not know!

The customer rang the Estate Office a week later, and spoke to Kates' manager. He said, 'I want to see that house again, but can I have a different agent please? I don't want to listen to that woman talking all the time!' The Manager took him out himself, he closed the sale the same day for 1.8 million.

If Kate had been actively listening to her customer, she would have taken him straight to that property and closed the sale within an hour of starting the assignment. Instead; all she got was a small split commission, as per agency policy.

Active listening is a skill to be valued. It is so easy to miss a subtle buying signal, or a vital clue to your customers needs.

If a client is upset, and you need to placate them, the best way is to actively listen until they have run out of steam. Get the whole story and the pent up emotion, just let them let it all out. Once this happens, your client calms and you can begin a rational approach to finding a solution.

I usually keep asking ' Is that the whole story?' which often sets the client off again, until they really have got it off the chest. Never argue with a client, even when they are completely wrong, even when it is not really your fault.

Accept total responsibility, remember, and then try to rationalise a solution. A huge part of getting to a point where you can not only salvage a client from the brink of throwing you out as a supplier, but even turn them into one of your most supportive clients instead, is the ability to actively listen to what they are telling you!

A critical element is that the client sees, feels and hears that you are actively listening. Active listening should be developed as a habit, and if you do this, you will be very happy with the rewards in your personal life as well.

You will be a far stronger negotiator, you will win more in every way including respect, and you will also know and understand more about most things in which you are engaged.

You can develop this habit, by actually stopping yourself every time someone talks to you for the next four weeks. Stop whatever else you are doing, or thinking, and focus on what they are saying to you.

Make yourself comment in a relevant way and take an interest. If someone talks to you at a time when you cannot stop and listen, explain this and arrange a suitable time to get back to them when you can listen.

If you make a conscious effort to do this all day, every day for four weeks, you will be well on your way to developing a new unconscious habit. Slowly you can then begin to resume normal patterns, except you retain the listening part, and you will find you can walk and listen, drive and listen or listen between events or appointments. It will become second nature.

The next time you see that same person, try and recall what their previous message was, and if appropriate refer to it. This reinforces listening skills for you, and shows them you really heard them.

You will identify and respond to buyer motivation much easier and faster if you can actively listen.

Questioning Techniques

The next skill we should enhance if we want to perform at the top of our profession is brilliant questioning techniques. Don't worry we are not going back to Sales 101, we are going to consider how to improve on those cliché open ended questions that we learnt years ago, but rarely use now because they sound exactly that – cliché

We do all know to ask open ended questions every time, yet I hear closed questions more than 50% of the time from top potential sales people. Why? In the heat of the enthusiasm, and in the pursuit of time, we forget!

Again it is kind of an art form to ask questions in a way that the person responding cannot help but give you an answer.

First we have to be in their shoes, and think about how they feel. Our clients may not want to be directly questioned, it may make them feel uncomfortable. Plus if we place our clients 'under fire' they begin to feel bored, or intimidated, and may respond with silly answers as a pay back. All of this needs to be avoided of course.

We need to weave our questions softly into a conversation that strengthens our connection. Our questions need to show interest in the broader scheme of things, whilst we can piece together or calculate their answers to more basic questions.

If I want to know what you earn, if I ask you directly you may feel offended or that it is none of my business. However I am sure we can both think of hundreds of questions we could ask that will give us an answer close enough for our purposes. If I want to know this, it is likely because I am trying to see if you can afford my offer, or I want to see where you fit in a hierarchy.

Let us use the suit as an example again.

If you ask me how much I earn, I will not tell you. I may not want to say how much I want to pay.

You could however, weave into conversation and draw out what brands I normally buy, what fabrics I prefer. Whether I say I buy Woolworths, or I say Armani, will give you the answer you need. Now I can wear Armani and be unable to afford food, but again that comes back to the right questions to give you the information you need. Multiple questions, asked in a subtle way, over a period of time allow you to cross check, and reference any discrepancies in my answers.

Try to make your questions as obscure as possible. Do not ask how much I earn, or what job I do, or where I work.....they are all too obvious. Take a more strategic approach, think about discussions we could have where I may voluntarily tell you my job, my company or indicate my income bracket.

So rather than front your clients with questions, try to weave them so softly into a discussion that they almost do notice them. Sales Legends have an ability to get people to tell them almost anything they want to know. Their questioning techniques are non-confrontational, soft and appear as subtle as a feather floating past.

They show interest by actively listening, and asking questions related to what their client just said, thus guiding their client across a floor well waxed and enabling a human connection that reminds me of an elegant waltz!

Both parties enjoy the flow of conversation, even if it is mostly the client talking. As we acknowledged earlier, people actually do like to talk and you can be considered a profound and intelligent conversationalist just by listening.

Questions should always be approached from a point of interest and respect. If you keep this predominantly in mind, your questioning should become a powerful tool.

> *I know someone who is always called when people need information in her company, she has the most amazing way of getting people to tell her exactly what she needs to know. You hardly hear her questions, yet her audience just spills over the edge like a waterfall. She has a way of making everyone feel comfortable and relaxed, and then the questions seem so innocent somehow.*

Her technique is ideal, the client talks to her in a conversational environment that feels relaxed and inviting. The feedback from any client is always that she is a warm, and amazing person! They trust her intuitively.

Before a meeting, have clearly defined the answers you need to get, and then let the conversation flow whilst gently guiding the direction to where those answers lie. Be patient, the more valuable the piece of information you need, the more difficult it will be. It will be well guarded and you will have to pay the price of time and sensitivity to get your answer. The more you have become a trusted adviser the easier it will be!

Negotiating Without Pain

Many sales campaigns go very well until the final stage of negotiation, when the ability to negotiate the fine points of a contract can become bogged or even broken. This often deteriorates the winning feeling in both the client and the salesperson, into almost a feeling of conflict, or combat.

A Sales Legend normally excels in negotiation. They are aware of the need to manage their sale beyond the booking, and into the contract phase, without taking their eyes off the ball. You do not score a goal, if the ball is not between the posts and out of play. Intensity of ill feeling that can be generated through these final stages can damage the future relationship with the client. If their lawyers and your lawyers are fighting, that impacts your day and your buyers day, it is frustrating for all. If the finance agreement is not in place, you can lose a closed deal. If the contract is not signed, or the PO not received, then you still do not have a win!

Ensuring these last stages are smoothly transacted will delight your customer, and increase their enthusiasm for working with you.

Once you have established you can win your deal, then to increase customer enthusiasm start to pave the way for a smooth final negotiation by checking standard contract conditions, by ensuring the financial path is clear and by having a good understanding of what final discounts, pricing and service elements will be needed.

This will unlikely be the first time this buyer, and this company, has bought a solution. There will be a track record of process and both positive and negative feedback associated. You can use your questioning techniques, and wolf-like demeanour, to find plenty of people who will tell you about previous contracts, or projects. You will know what to expect, therefore have an armada of tactics ready for the negotiating table.

Negotiating is all about give and take, and generating a feeling of both sides having won. The buyer wins because they have the best solution at a very fair price, the seller wins because they have another sale in the bag at expected profitability ratios. Negotiations turn sour when one party feels that they are no longer winning, but instead they lose ground.

It is possible in negotiation to look at what benefits or services are not required in the contract to meet the budget of a client. It is a cool idea to ask your client to help you close the price gap. Let us assume you have a 100k gap on a deal worth 1m, your client is only willing to pay 900k. Now that is a big difference of 10%. So sit with your client, explain your inability to meet that gap as is, however ask them to help you find out how the budget could be met. Sometimes, they will admit it is purely a budget issue, but a different way of handling the contract will move some of the funding into a different budget.

Perhaps you have a competitor who has offered a solution 100k cheaper than you can, yet the client has still chosen your solution, so identify why and use that as a strength in your negotiation. You will still likely have to 'give' something, but maybe that can be a discount on future upgrades, or an additional service for a trial period, or another product that costs you little.

Negotiation must remain respectful at all times, and where possible introduce some soft humour or lightness to the meetings. People who feel relaxed and comfortable will give way more than those who 'sense' the importance of the occasion. Refer always to the issues surrounding the contract and your companys' ability to meet criteria, and never make any discussion personal. Neither party is right, or wrong! It is just difference in the way they view the same proposal. Negotiation will run smoother if you maintain phenomenal human connections, and make the issues non-personal.

Be unafraid to ask for what you need, and to do this as a suggestion when introduced. Frame everything in terms of meeting client business needs. Be aware of what strength you really have, and try as much as possible to avoid closures at end of your quarter, or measurable quota period. The traditional hockey stick at the end of each sale period puts increased pressure on any negotiation, and is giving your client a position of too much strength, and they will use it. So they should. If you are going to have to negotiate on closing days, then try to have as much agreed and documented prior to the final decision as you possibly can. That way the PO process will be smoother.

Heated moments increase tensions, and you will tend to give more than you needed to. A Sales Legend will avoid this situation.

> *I worked for a large software company. The SVP liked to have all salespeople around in the closing hours of the quarter, late into the evening.*
>
> *One quarter, I had exceeded my numbers and closed all possible business a few days before quarter end. The SVP*

was upset because I was not stressing at the close with many others. He did not seem to understand that he should have been pleased that my POs were not in the system at the 11th hour, and my profitability was higher, but he seemed to think I was negligent not to have orders at the close stage.

Sometimes, Sales Leadership needs to put more significance on closing deals earlier. They have become so familiar with the hockey stick, that despite despising it, they actually foster its growth.

Win/win negotiation is a strength commonly associated with Sales Legends.

The only Legend I have ever met who was not a strong negotiator used to pay the costs of a skilled negotiator, he trusted, to do this for him. His clients were aware of this, and accepted his eccentricity. His clients knew and understood he did not have the ability to focus on the detail of a contract, but his human connection and ability to generate customer enthusiasm was so fantastic that no one ever minded, in fact it added to his legend!

Being In The Moment

Sales Legends are not easily distracted, they are memorable because they are in the moment.

We have reviewed in this chapter both active listening and passive questioning. Now they can effectively come together, to make a strong human connection, by ensuring you are always residing in the moment.

It is better to truly listen to someone for five minutes then excuse yourself, than to only partially hear them for twenty minutes.

Remember, to help yourself stay focussed by acknowledging and visualizing what the person is talking about, give regular verbal signals that you are listening. If you don't want to prolong the conversation, then never interrupt, if you just truly listen, the talker runs out of things to say, much faster than if engaged in discussion.

Now for the final stroke of genius - When you leave your audience, ensure they have a statement from you that rewards them. Never leave without making such a gesture. You must leave your client with a feeling of satisfaction, that his or her time was very well regarded.

It could be as simple as 'It was fabulous we had this chance to meet' or 'Thank you for sharing that with me, I find this useful input' and if relevant 'I will certainly get back to you on this' (and make 100% sure that you do!).

This simple practice of demonstrating you are engaged with your audience, 'in the moment of time', will place you in a category apart from your peers very quickly. It is a rare, but highly valued ethic – to show you are' in the moment'.

Customers and employees, in fact any audience, will say you are an engaging speaker, fabulous to talk to, 'had a most interesting conversation with him/her'

Actually, maybe you didn't even have a conversation, it was more of a listening, but people so like to speak about themselves that they can easily forget you didn't say very much!

Being In the Moment, you will remember that Communication is not a competition. It enhances customer enthusiasm and is a very delicate part of making a memorable human connection.

IPI for the VIP

An enthusiastic customer is the greatest ally and promoter of any salesperson.

All our customers are people, they all have emotions and feelings, families and friends, pets, sports, hobbies and interests. They feel good if you remember important personal information they tell you.

Connecting with them on a personal level is a way to enthuse our customers about seeing us again. To have them see us and want to come and chat to us in the café, or at the football, or in the mall indicates we have made a strong connection that extends beyond the workplace.

If they only recognize you in your suit, then you need to reassess your connection!

When they see you, and come and chat to you at an industry event, you can see, feel and often hear the reaction of your competitors. Witnessing a flurry of exchanged looks, whispers and positioning on a competitive show stand can be a lot of fun.

It is therefore important to remember any important personal information they have imparted to you. If they introduced you to their wife, it is pertinent to send her your regards each time you see your customer. If they told you their daughter was a finalist in a law scholarship, then you need to be interested enough to ask how that went. If she told you her husband was buying a new car, remember to check if he was enjoying it.

If they told you they were about to be divorced, or their partner left them, or some other very delicate personal detail. Leave it alone, but do check in a generic way how they are going. Ensure this is always in a private moment. Reassure them they are looking great, or empathise with their need for a break. You will have to call these ones on the fly, but try to avoid hearing all the ugly intimate details, it could compromise your relationship.

Try and remember they do not like coffee, are allergic to shellfish, have a pet hatred of red walls, or any other detail you have found out. Their birthday is a nice one to remember, few suppliers do this, and it is always nice to receive a small simple card in the mail, or an email. It is positively memorable to a client that you actively listened, and you cared enough to remember them as a person, not just a CIO or VP Engineering for your client company.

The last thing you want is that your boss takes them to a seafood restaurant, or a meeting room with red walls, so this is important briefing information for anyone in your organization that meets them. Too few salespeople provide this in the briefing document. There is nothing more embarrassing for your Sales Leader than if, just as they are about to usher your client into a nice wine bar, they say ' I am surprised Joe didn't tell you I don't drink alcohol.'

If you see them in social situations, with your family, then you better also brief your family what to avoid.

It is positive if your partner says, 'Joe tells me you grow award winning roses' but not if they say 'Joe tells me you hate dogs, why is that?' or 'Joe said you are fighting for custody of your kids' These things are best left well alone by you, and those associated to you!

If you have a crap memory, train it or make notes for yourself.

Personal information is power. The power to use it, to generate a better connection, and customer enthusiasm. Conversely, also the power to destroy your relationship in a single sentence!

Respect, Appreciation and Availability.

One of the ways to generate customer enthusiasm is if they see, hear and feel your respect for them. If you behave respectfully towards them, then walk out and raise your eyes to the ceiling in front of the receptionist and comment to a colleague 'What a dick!' Then you will likely find your respect is neither believed nor appreciated. You have been exposed as a fake!

If you have trouble respecting your client, find things about them you can respect and focus on them. Keep your opinions to yourself, and only express the positive, or what you would say in front of them.

Sales Legends are known to defend their clients by focusing on the positive. An example might be a comment from a colleague ' Wow, that guy is a terrible dresser, did you see his tie?' Response could be ' I don't care what he wears, he is a very competent engineer and he has power to decide which supplier wins the new system.' Thus reinforcing your own respect, whilst also teaching your team respect for the client at all times. Your client will never hear that you said anything negative about him or her. In the end your colleagues will stop the negative comments.

If we make respect, even at our own ego cost, to be a habit we will not slip up by agreeing with a competitive colleague that actually the buyer is a dick!

If we respect our client, then it will be easy to appreciate the information they give us, the time they make available, and most of all the orders we receive. Let's be honest here, that is why we are there at all – to gain business. It is also important that we show we appreciate all these things, and not just the order. It makes sense to come from a position of gratitude. Always thank them for their time. Tell them regularly that you appreciate their support and their business. Too few salespeople can do this. An order received is an order forgotten quickly, but maybe it saved your arse last quarter.

From respecting and appreciating your client, their time and support, comes the concept of availability. A Sales Legend is almost always available to their clients. They move internal events to facilitate necessary meetings in the clients timeframe, not their own. They will drive across town, rather than say 'I am not around that day, how about next week?'

If you have to tell a client you are not available it is a dampener to their enthusiasm. If you are with another client, then you need to make time available as soon as possible that fits with his agenda, or decide if it is appropriate to send someone else on your behalf.

Now, if you have a client (and it does happen) who likes to exercise his power by calling you at midnight on Saturday, when it is not urgent, then you will need to protect yourself without damaging his enthusiasm. At reasonable times, turn off your phone and check messages regularly or set expectations up front of the times you consider you cannot be available. I always tell clients well ahead of any planned vacation, or other time out such as training, long meetings etc. I always put someone in place to handle issues that may arise, or contact me if urgent.

Clients understand this, and are generally happy if they can contact someone who will help them, or has access to you if it is really important. I have been on the receiving end of phone calls from frustrated clients who were unable to get assistance during a sales kick-off, or an 'off site'.

They had no problem that their sales executive was not available, but were frustrated that no contingency plan was in place during their absence.

Make yourself available to your customers, set expectations in advance and always ensure they can find someone relevant in an emergency.

This will contribute to having an enthusiastic customer.

Presentations

This is really important. Death by PowerPoint is still a Death!

Please, please be prudent and rational about your presentations. Most presentations are frankly boring. You may only have to sit through your own, but your client may have to sit through several on a short list. All saying the same:

- We are the leading company
- Irrelevant organisation details
- Feature, Feature, Feature and occasionally an attempt at a few benefits
- Meaningless generic technical diagrams that do not link to the business needs
- Endless extended versions of above
- A Written version of what is presented

Rarely do we see a crisp presentation of what the customer is actually interested in:

- How stable are you financially
- How Experienced are you?
- Do You understand my business, my project and its relevance?
- How will you support us?
- Show me the relevance of your solution to my business needs
- What else can I do with this solution?
- The Future and Lifespan?
- Can you meet my deadlines and my budget?

Keep business level presentations as short as possible. I once saw a final customer presentation, for a fairly straightforward solution, of 120 slides! I asked the salesperson to go away and reduce it to a maximum of 15!

Sales Legends are entertaining presenters, who can get their key messages **remembered** without boring their audience. If you are not, then this is something that you either work hard on changing, or you minimize your part to an opening and a close, and find great presenters from your team.

Try and isolate technical presentations for technical audiences, but present both business benefits and technology relevance to technical audiences.

Amanda Fleming, is an extraordinary keynote speaker from Auckland in New Zealand. She is a presenter for whom I have the utmost respect as a powerhouse of energy on stage, and she is certainly memorable! I was privileged to have her as our team coach and she taught us that 93% of the message is the messenger! Only 7% is the message itself, so stick to key points and use those NLP skills we overviewed in the Human Connection to ensure everyone remembers it.

There are some fabulous presentation courses available in various parts of the world, but look for the more radical ones, do not do any course called 'Presentation Skills' The title already threatens to bore a passionate, attention deficit, high powered sales person before they even get there! Don't bother with courses that tell you how to stand, how to look, and how to present – because then you focus on those techniques, instead of your message.

Look for courses that show you how to be you, relaxed and happy on stage regardless of the size of your audience, and confidently delivering a message they remember.

Another wonderful quote I must share with you from Amanda Fleming is 'If your butt is itchy, then scratch it, no one will even notice!'

Her belief was if you stand there, uncomfortably wriggling instead, it will show on your face that you are distracted by something and you will lose your vital connection.

Great presenters have a natural advantage over other sales people, so it is worth the effort to excel in your presentations and enthuse your customers.

Ask and Tell

The final technique in the effort to excite your customer, and encourage them to be enthusiastic about you, is the Ask and Tell tactic.

This is for when you win, and will help your customer remember what an amazing salesperson you really are!

Ask your customer what you could have done better, how could you have made it easier for them in the sales process?

You may be rewarded, after a great campaign, with a compliment that you did everything right. More importantly though, this is a chance to show humility even in the glow of the win, and maybe learn something that will help you win more in the future!

Don't waste this valuable chance to do two things:

- Learn something valuable
- Demonstrate what a Legend you really are!

Tell every person in your client, with whom you interfaced in the campaign, how much you appreciate the business. This like any thank you, is always appreciated and remembered. All those people were part of your campaign, thank your enemies too, maybe you can convert them to supporters!

Legends Secret Number Six

This might sound so simple that you cannot imagine why I would list it as a Legends Secret. It is so powerful, yet it is very rarely executed.

There is one other time you can effectively use a different version of the **Tell** technique, but this must be executed only once, and with the timing and precision of a surgical laser.

In your closing statement, at the final presentation, you can tell the audience that you really want their business.

> *I used this tactic in a huge and highly competitive bid presentation. The contenders to win were close in value, in solution, in capability. I needed one last advantage. I told the Board, 'It matters to us that we win your business. We believe we have the right solution that meets your business requirements, we have the capability to meet your deadlines, we have a team of talented, experienced people who will delight your people in delivery, and above all we will value your trust in us and never let you down'.*
>
> *I got an applause, and my salesperson was aggravated after the presentation, he demanded to know why did I show my hand about how much winning meant to us, where was my pride?*
>
> *I said, 'Does it matter if we win?' 'Of Course' he said, 'Well then all I did was tell the truth, let's see what happens'*
>
> *We won. A few days later the CIO called me personally to tell me no one had ever done that before, and his Board very much appreciated the integrity and honesty. They believed, if*

> the General Manager would say that, then I represented a company culture they could count on.

Probably scary, but it is a powerful closing tactic if used with a statement appropriate to the audience.

Never waste this by using it too early, or too often or on too many people. This is for the final decision making team only.

"Sales Legends are known to defend their clients by focussing on the positive."

Networking and Reputation

Networking and Reputation

The Sales Legend is always working on personal, and business, networks to be truly connected.

On the business level they will be incisive in knowing who really matters, no matter what level they are in society, the workplace, or demographically.

They are great listeners, yet only speak of things that interest their audiences. They inspire people with passion, energy and personal charisma. They will hear the rumbles of the underground but never engage in idle gossip.

They often enjoy a good sense of humour and demonstrate high levels of tolerance. They are trusted by their company and their clients.

They will protect and grow their reputation, even taking it as far as building a personal brand.

A Sales Legend knows that who they are, and who they are perceived to be, will dictate the level of access they can enjoy and the doors that are open to them.

Your reputation often precedes you, particularly in the houses of power and influence.

Ensure Your Reputation is Solid.

A Salespersons success and, to a large degree, their future career will be dictated by one thing only – their reputation. It is a profession where reputation matters more than most other professions.

Doors are opened to you based on your reputation. You receive job offers based upon your reputation. You will be promoted or fired based upon your reputation (of course, your numbers also form part of your reputation). You will receive management support relative to your reputation.

Thus a salesperson must protect and build their reputation as a priority in their lives.

There is no PhD in selling. If you damage your reputation, or built a poor one to begin with, then you will suffer as you cannot just go and prove yourself with a higher degree!

Reputation is particularly important, as selling is a social career, you must depend on other people to achieve anything. It is your skill as the master of the matrix, to bring everyone together to achieve a successful sale.

We already understand what you need to be known for, so that you stand above the rest. You need to be approachable, humble yet passionate, and exude a warm charismatic persona. You need to be focussed on winning, and be willing to take total responsibility and follow up every one and every action, every step of the way. Yet, you must do this in a way that does not cause offence. People like to spend time with you because you are respectful, and you show this by actively listening and delivering your messages in an intelligent and engaging way. You really connect with people.

You understand and use the Law of Attraction to your advantage, you spend one minute more with everyone you meet, you astound people with your campaign strategy and regularly leave your competitors agog! You are known to be a trusted adviser to your clients, a truly professional sales person.

You are either a Sales Legend, or becoming one!

This puts you amongst the top 5% of your profession. You need to protect this reputation at all cost.

This means that you need to manage yourself, so that you do not do anything too stupid, at any time, that will destroy what you have built. This does not mean you have to be perfect. Perfect is pretty boring and irritating to most people. It does mean however, that you do know when to draw the line and pull back from the brink of criticism. This is particularly important when you are anywhere that your behaviour can be observed by colleagues or clients. However, it is a good habit to develop generally.

Let me try and convey exactly what I mean here. This does not mean you may not enjoy a few drinks, or do wild and fun things, or be adventurous. It does mean that you do not fall drunken in the street, or vomit anywhere but an appropriate place. Stay away from illegal drug usage, even if you know your client indulges. Never take part in anything that compromises you or your client!

Now, I am not saying this because I am a 'girl', or because I am being boring – if you check my reputation you will hear that actually I am a bit of a wild child!

I am saying this because, we are no longer living and working in an environment where behaviour like this is acceptable to companies, or government organizations. People, including client employees, get fired for compromising their company's reputation, or if in the public sector, for behaviour that could be criticized by the public.

Pre 1995, subject to cultural restrictions, you could probably take your client to a brothel, get very drunk together, streak at the football and it may all have been considered a good laugh! Today, that has changed. High level salespeople just do not go there anymore, because integrity and respect are now accepted business ethics, and even fashionable!

Sales Kick Offs were notorious for salespeople behaving badly in the name of fun, and if you had good enough numbers, maybe you got away with it. In 2010 and the foreseeable beyond, you will not. You will also damage your reputation. You will unlikely have access to the corridors of power, you will be considered a loser.

Colleagues are more competitive than ever, as employment becomes less available and reputations become more important. People will go after you, even if before they did not have a reason to. I do not condone this, or say that it is good, it is just cold, hard fact.

> *I have a colleague who is a Senior Manager in Sales Operations. I respect him enormously but he damaged his reputation and his career at a recent kickoff event.*
>
> *On the second evening, of the event, Aaron had quite a few drinks, then a few other senior colleagues decided to carry on even later at another club downtown. Aaron stayed out drinking until nearly 5am.*
>
> *He had to give a presentation on a sales program the next morning at 9am. To give Aaron credit, he arrived at 8.45am appropriately dressed and gave a flawless, albeit a bit lower energy presentation, on time.*
>
> *Julie, a colleague from another region who worked for an associated department, came up to Aaron and was very upset. She told him ' You should be embarrassed, your presentation was ok but your eyes are red and you smell of*

alcohol. You looked tired and hung over on stage, I don't believe you showed respect for our global sales teams presenting in such condition.'

Aaron was angry because he felt he had done his bit. He knew he had played hard, but he also knew he was there on time and delivered. He believed his colleagues should understand that it was kickoff, and many senior people had also been out late, including his Senior Vice President. It was behaviour that a few years ago, would have been a funny 'bad boy story' but in 2009 just didn't fly anymore.

I was not there, so I cannot decide who was right or wrong, and in the end it doesn't matter. Aaron badly damaged his reputation that morning and Julie, his colleague who complained, actually blew this up into a big issue by communicating to many her disgust.

Aaron eventually decided to change roles, and try to rebuild a professional reputation in another department. Such was the damage of a few colleagues noticing, and taking issue, that he was not in prime condition to deliver his presentation.

Now, no matter how we think about this issue and whether you side with Julie or Aaron, it was Aaron whose career has suffered a major setback!

He forgot to guard his reputation on that one evening and a colleague was offended by what she perceived as a lack of respect. This turned into an incident that involved management, HR and cross border gossip and rivalry. The management, in this case did little, as it was not seen as misconduct.

> *I tried to help Aaron repair the damage by suggesting an apology be sent to Julie and her peers, but in the end Aarons career still suffered and there is a note of the incident on his HR file!*
>
> *Some colleagues in the company now perceive him as less senior, or try to avoid him. The old, tribal custom of 'stay away from a tainted person'. This is the only, less than exemplary, thing Aaron ever did, yet I have heard other senior colleagues imply that he is a bit of a loser. Now that is not the truth, Aaron is a committed, enthusiastic achiever in his job, but one who has a damaged reputation that is hard to rebuild.*

One could contend that it is a shame the fun side of work hard, play hard is vanishing from the workplace but regardless of our opinions one way or another, acceptable behaviour to maintain a good reputation has dramatically changed in just a decade or so.

I am still a bit of a wild child inside, but I understand that in 2010 and beyond I have to manage that wild child much more responsibly than ever before. My reputation opens too many doors for me, even out of curiosity!

So to be a Sales Legend, you will need to fiercely protect your reputation and beware not to slip up occasionally. Your successful career depends on it now!

Pre-Empt Any Negative Feedback

If you have something in your background that you know can be used against you, then you need to pre-empt it with people you wish to influence.

> *I have a friend who is a CEO and President of Sales. He has a very wild personal history, but it was primarily based in the 80s and 90s when what he did was considered funny, and he was definitely a 'Jack the Lad' There are a few legends around some of the outrageous things he did, and deals that he won etc.*
>
> *He is intelligent enough to know that today he has to change this behaviour, and he has certainly toned it down. He has a huge cynical sense of humour and he uses this to pre-empt any negative feedback his competitors can use against him.*
>
> *He is divorced, with a few kids that he just adores. His personal life can be somewhat colourful at times and each personal story is leaked into his work environment, usually an enhanced version by competitors.*
>
> *He now pre-empts all of this with clients. he comes right out, up front and with his engaging honesty he just disarms any weapon his competitors may try to use. So with a combination, of less stories and his pre-emptive handling of the matter, he remains a true Sales Legend.*
>
> *I heard him say to a new client at a dinner party recently, "Yeah, you probably heard about me, I am the one with ten wives, fifteen kids and a fleet of expensive Italian cars" Huge smile, and then he removes any embarrassment by adding "actually the story is much more boring, I have one ex-wife, four kids that I am very proud of, and actually I drive a*

> *Mazda! But hey don't tell anyone, you will spoil my image'"*
> *Another huge smile. The whole issue just goes away.*

How you pre-empt your situation, if you have one, will be something you will have to consider personally, and handle quickly and efficiently each time you engage a new client, or person of influence.

When you are witness to clients behaving badly. If possible depart the situation with a valid excuse. If you can't, unless it is something highly illegal, then develop a poor memory for anything you saw and try not to compromise yourself. Never refer to it with your client again. If you are in the position of something very illegal, that also compromises you, you must get out or your whole career can go down! I have witnessed that no client, and no job, is worth that.

So, next time you are in for a wild ride, consider carefully the risks before committing your future on the line. Above all, remember from this day forward, build and protect your reputation as a professional, and as a trusted human being, if you want to be a Sales Legend.

Know Who Matters. Engage When Possible

In any client, there will be a list of people who are important to you. You need to be sure you recognise the most important influencers by researching and finding pictures of key figures and memorise the faces. Then you can ensure you are smiling, greeting them by name and being particularly courteous if you happen to bump into them somewhere.

If it is the CEO, you should not, as we discussed earlier, launch into your elevator pitch. Instead ensure that you are noticed and remembered in a positive way. You do not want to be the person who drove past and splashed his suit with rainwater, or rushed ahead of him into the lift! You want to be the one who greeted him by name, asked him an intelligent question, or wished him a great day.

You can introduce yourself with a simple explanation such as '*Good Morning, Mr Beams. It is a pleasure to meet you. I am Sandra Williams, and I am visiting Joe Barnes today to discuss the new networking project.*' Then shut up, listen actively and see if he asks you anything. Respond positively and briefly, wish him a great day and get on with your business.

Mr Beams, CEO, will recall that encounter positively, and that is all you need in such an informal situation. It may be that you get an invitation to brief him, or maybe not. Go with the flow, but in 2010 it is not trendy to push senior executives with aggressive sales tactics.

Listen, Listen, Listen

This is a short reiteration of the active listening technique as applied to your reputation and networking. Having developed this skill to listen to clients, hopefully you chose to also deploy it throughout your life. If is most effective as a holistic life habit, because this will truly enhance your reputation as a great conversationalist!

To have the reputation of someone who really listens to people is an attractive proposition to anyone who may want to engage someone in your position. You will attract additional opportunities when you have a reputation as an engaging communicator.

You will be told more, you will hear everything. You will know more than others and you will know what your competitors are doing. You will develop the ability to store small snippets of information, that automatically attach themselves to other pertinent snippets of information, heard at a later time. These information strings eventually form cohesive patterns that expose information you may need. This may be information you will never receive any other way, due to client staffs' awareness of need for discretion.

Because you listen actively, people will find you interesting to talk to. They will tell you more than you can believe was ever possible. Confidentiality is essential, like a great journalist, never reveal your sources. Just listen, file, and later reconstruct.

Engaging The Competitor

Whenever possible engage your competitors at appropriate opportunities, unless prohibited to do so by regulatory issues covering your industry, or the particular opportunity. For example some high level defence bids strictly prohibit vendors communicating during the bid process.

This is best done publicly, so that no coercion or inappropriate cooperation can be inferred. Ideal times are industry events, trade shows or social occasions. Be very aware of discussing anything that could breach governance such as discounts, price, value etc. Avoid one on ones in obscure places, you could be compromised even though you did nothing. You should not actively engage a competitor during a sales campaign, you should only actively seek co-incidental meetings.' What a coincidence that they are here too! `

If you can allow your competitor to talk, even to brag, then you may uncover a bullet to use later. Remember, they may also be 999ers, and may feed you misinformation to deflect your attention or distract you. Listen actively, contribute little , and you may uncover vital intelligence to enhance your campaign strategy.

You can use your ability to distract, or you can practise your language skills by creating elegant statements that sound wonderful but mean absolutely nothing.

If you have ever watched an episode of the BBC's 'Yes Minister' you will have already learnt a lot about this art from Humphrey! If you haven't see it, buy the DVD and watch a few episodes, at worst you have a good laugh, but at best you will learn how to talk to a competitor and reveal nothing!

Hear The Rumble Of The Underground

It is good to be aware of what is being said ' around the traps', and in the industry in general about you, the campaigns you work on, and your clients.

You need to be informed if there are rumours of poor financial performance in your client, you do not want to win because you are the only one stupid enough to still supply a client who cannot pay.

You need to know if someone is spreading a bad rumour about you, your campaign or your company. You need to know if your client has customers who are complaining about poor service, perhaps this opens new opportunity for you to enhance this clients' ability to improve process.

You also need to know if your competitor has done something that compromises them, and you just gained an advantage.

There are hundreds of other useful pieces of information you can use in your campaigns, and to develop more business.

To hear the underground you need to be well connected. This means a sound reputation, but even more a great network of contacts. The bigger your network, both personal and professional, the more you will know. Sometimes it is someone connected via your childs' school, or your local DIY, or your hairdresser that will give you a vital piece of information that helps, or protects, you.

A large network is also very useful when you want to form a Consortium, or find a good lawyer, or need a top consultant, or just an introduction - in fact any support or information.

999 would never leave the ground if it were not for my personal network of people who believe in me, and in what I am doing. These connections open doors for me, and offer all forms of unforseen assistance, support, new connections and events that I never dreamed would come my way.

My network is a connective matrix of energy that works like the blood that flows in my veins and connects, and feeds, my vital organs. Without my network I am nothing but a solo being, alone on a very large, and often dangerous planet. My network protects me, encourages me, challenges me, and is the most significant part of my success. It is built from so many of the elements we have discussed – human connection, one minute more; Law of Attraction, reputation, passion, energy and a genuine respect for those with whom I connect.

Building A Personal Brand

Sales Legends are like a personal brand. It is possible to hear a statement like ' I am going to use a Williams technique' perhaps referring to a legendary tactic used in a deal closed by Williams.

It is not just in Sales Legends but all types of legends. Think of Microsoft and a lot of people immediately make a comment about 'Gates.' Like him, or hate him, does not matter, Bill Gates is truly a legend. Bill Gates is a brand that represents the small guy who made it to the top of the worlds industry from a start in his garage.

The founders of Hewlett Packard are also legends, with even stronger branding than Gates. In 1938 they rented the garage from their landlady and started what has become an industry giant. A household, and enterprise brand, that even today carries only the name of the two legends who started the company.

On a much smaller scale every Sales Legend can become a personal brand. People in your region, and your industry, will know what that name is associated with. Sometimes in the CEO space, you will see a companys' share price rise, or fall, on the appointment of a legendary branded CEO. I have also seen this in Sales, when a particularly high achieving salesperson or sales leader is hired for a very significant client.

Business headlines like ' Acme Hires Williams' or 'Acme loses Williams to Thobis' can affect a share price! This is when a sales person has reached the top of the legend ladder!

If you aspire to become a Sales Legend, then consider building a personal brand at the same time.

What happens when you type in your name on Google?

If you want to be a legend, then you can think about how you would like your name to appear. Legends usually appear on the front page, and there are links to their name from many independent sources.

Is it worthwhile to start with a simple website that tells people who you are? Do you use Social Networking to enhance your image? Can you publish articles on the internet that help other sales people, or interesting stories to entertain people? Are you listed in professional directories with an up to date photo and information. Can you establish yourself as a trusted business adviser, and solution provider, to a vertical, or an industry?

Personal branding is a great way to build your career and your reputation, if you can be found quickly on a search, you will gain credibility and your reputation will build even faster.

Building a consistent personal brand, and reputation, offline and online is highly recommended for any aspiring Sales Legends.

A SALES LEGEND IS A GREAT COMMUNICATOR WHO CONNECTS AT EVERY LEVEL.

Art Of Replication

Art of Replication

The Sales Legend will win, win and win again. Astounding everyone, thus establishing the legend.

They will acknowledge the great race their competitors ran, and show their respect for them.

They will always be working on an Overlap Engagement model, and rarely engage in domino models.

What differentiates these legends from the rest of us?

As we have discussed before, they are first and foremost trusted advisers, and often Wolves, inside their own organisations and their customers organisation. They have earnt this position through diligent application of the elements we have discussed in this guide.

They work on an overlap engagement model, in that whilst they are campaigning for a particular project, they are already using their matrix maximisation to uncover and start developing the next engagement/s.

Often they are working on several campaigns, or projects, within their client simultaneously. They do not take their eye off the ballpark, and allow a competitor to gain a foothold through the door via a project they were unaware of.

They run campaigns of high integrity, maintaining total accountability before and after the sale. They ensure every part of delivery is meeting with the clients' expectation before and after the deal is won. Understanding that post sale attitude and delivery impact their ability to win again.

The Sales Legend is never a hit and run advocate.

There are common stories about sales people who are not seen between an order for the last project, until the new project is announced. They are considered just pure hunters, combing the field of opportunity in order to be fed.

A Sales Legend has a different approach, he or she is a business developer (little bit farmer, little bit hunter and a lot the environmentalist) and knows that a continuous relationship with a client is necessary to maintain a strong position when a campaign arises. They are usually seen to be part of the initiation of new projects and ideas for which they can provide solutions. They are seen at client industry events, to learn about the industry and direction of their clients business.

Just like the wolf, they know their territory intimately, and do not abuse it. They hunt to eat, yet respect every other creature within the space, as each plays their role in helping the wolf. The owl tells him what she sees, the eagle spots a fast rabbit heading the way of the wolf, and each individual is part of the eco-system for the good of the forest. This analogy is the territory of the Sales Legend, they are using all their habits, skills and intelligence to see where they could assist their clients improve their business with their solutions and services. This is a perfect symbiotic client – supplier relationship.

They patrol their territory by walking the floor, talking the talk, both in their clients and their own company. They demonstrate respect, sensitivity, empathy and intelligence as they contribute to the improvement of their own services and delivery.

They are in touch with their networks, and hear the rumble of the underground, alerting them to dangerous situations, traps and new opportunities.

They remain consistent in their clients, and rest only a very short time after each win, knowing that they can apply their boundless energy again and again.

They treat every campaign as a unique one, going through all the same qualification steps, asking "Can I win? Will I win? Do I have the resources? What is the price and what else do I need?"

They do this to prevent complacency in themselves, because it is a threat to the future. They do it to prevent running a second class, or stale campaign, so that their competitors cannot predict their strategy.

They keep developing their network, and have at hand at all times potential partners willing to work with them, because they have a reputation as the best in class.

They know what they could have done better, and do it better. Every single document is improved every single time it is sent to a client, thus continuing to delight their customers.

They remember to thank everyone remotely involved in the previous win, if possible they do it personally.

They apply every piece of energy to developing new opportunity and keeping their competitors challenged.

Within the boundaries of their territory, if appropriate they are always seeking new contacts to build into new clients, and with a well executed strategic plan, destabilise existing competitors and their products.

They justify everything, to everyone on a business basis and never on features and benefits alone.

They absolutely know the difference between a benefit and a feature. Now whilst that may sound offensive, you may just be surprised how many of your colleagues still cannot identify a true benefit.

A benefit is only meaningful, if your client can perceive that he, or she, needs this benefit. So, what does it actually mean for their business.

Every day, I see presentations that say something like this:

Acme Mobile Solutions

Feature	Benefit
• 45 Ringtones	• Identify Your Calls
• Inbuilt Camera 6.0	• Crisp clear pictures
• X MG memory card	• Store more information

These benefits are not actually meaningful. The real benefit is not obvious. For example instead of saying 'Store more information' perhaps it could say 'Store up to 700 contacts' or 'Stores up to 500 sms' that may then be a benefit for me.

A CIO I interviewed for this book told me:

> *Last week, I had a sales person presenting a benefit slide. It was a waste of my time. I was buying a storage solution for our backups.*
>
> *They kept telling me how fast their solution was, and sold the benefit of cutting our back up time in half. It is a useless 'benefit' to me, we only do this production backup at 2am, when the network is empty and there are no other applications running. I do not care if it takes 30 minutes or 60 minutes; It is worth nothing to me. When I asked them why this was a benefit, they said it would save network costs and minimise outages... How is that possible in my environment?*
>
> *At no time was I told a compelling reason why I should buy their solution than any other one. I would pay more if someone did that, sold me a benefit that was actually a benefit to my business.*

Sales Legends are very compelling in their client scenarios, they know and can advise their clients exactly why they have a good solution!

Wasting the time of a CIO is a replication killer, he or she will not make time for you again.

Legends Secret Number Seven

This is a small and simple secret for replicating your success in a client.

Never stop asking how you can help.

Too simple to be a secret? No, it is rarely done.

In most cases, a sale is won, sales person vanishes for awhile and maybe periodically pops up to look through the window, or enjoy a coffee. Truly!

If you keep building your matrix, and ask everyone every time you see them, how you can help them – you will replicate success by winning lots of even small pieces of business that are never in a competitive situation.

Clients become very enthusiastic and loyal about a salesperson who remains constant through the relationship.

If you have several clients, then diary time every month for just visiting and looking for ways you can help your client excel and win through the application of whatever you have to sell. Not just the purchasing office, or your own supporter, but the business units, the production floors- how good is your relationship? If you are a trusted adviser you can do this, and you may even be invited by the C-level to become involved at the strategic level of suppliers.

The Art of Replication is taking that in which you have excelled and improving on it every time.

Taking what you have not done well and fixing it.

Ensuring that you develop all your projects on an overlap basis, so you have no time for downtime. Maintaining the same ownership, passion and energy levels for your clients at all times so that you can fence your perimeter from attack. Listening to your clients, the underground, your network and your team every day.

Acting like a Sales Legend in all things thus developing a consistent business model of sustainable high quality proposals and resultant business.

WHAT NOW?

What Now?

We said in the overview:

To become a Sales Legend you will need to continue to excel as a sales athlete, year after year. There are pitfalls to avoid, and behaviours to celebrate and continue. Self motivation techniques and ways to maintain your mind, and body, at peak performance.

We have discussed the behaviours one should celebrate to become a Sales Legend, and we have seen some pitfalls that lie in wait for sales people. You are now professionally armed with the knowledge of what differentiates a Sales Legend from a good sales person. Now it is up to you, to develop the habits, deploy the techniques collectively and of course practise using those 7 Legends Secrets daily.

Let's now look at some Self Motivation techniques and habits, as well as a few tips I can give you on how to maintain peak performance physically and mentally to avoid burn out. I would even like to help you rocket yourself out of down times within a few hours.

We understand that a Sales Legend is on fire, and they feed that fire daily.

But how?

The Daily Traps

Every day is riddled with traps to eat up our productive time, and give us excuses why we couldn't do what we should have done.

Communication is the first one. We now have to deal with a phone glued to our person pretty much 24 x 7, email that people expect answered immediately as though we had nothing else to do but sit at our pc, and email overload. If you work in IT, the email overload will be threatening like an avalanche. We live and work in an age where people operate primarily in one e-mode or another and expect that we do the same.

This needs managing or it will threaten your chances to be successful, but give you a thousand excuses - not much use for a Sales Legend.

Email and Phones

You can use a simple system for your email, even if you get hundreds every day. The secret is not to let that Inbox grow too large, or all is lost.

If it is too large, and overwhelming to even contemplate starting, then I suggest hitting the delete button (after a quick check for anyone critical on the list like your client, your boss, or the word URGENT). Then let everyone assume you had a hard drive failure, and you will probably be shocked that only about 10% of that original email ever comes back to you again ☺

Set up a simple set of files that are easy to store to....I suggest one for every month, plus a few identified for your main clients, or projects and the common reports you get every day, and may need to recall.

I have one file for each month, and then I have about 10 other folders for emails that I regularly need to recall, such as key clients, project data, regulatory notifications, sales competitions and product releases. Auto file, through using the filter rules option, everything that you can.

Everything on which you are CC'd can be filtered to a separate Inbox, you probably don't need to read most of it.

Every day, I open my email, I first delete or file things I don't need to open. There goes usually at least 50%.

Then I view and file every email appropriately, anything I cannot handle 'on the fly' I mark it, and leave it in my Inbox. i.e. Handle it and file it, or else leave it where I cannot forget it, this means only about 5% of my email needs to remain in my inbox!

Only check email at certain points of the day, do other stuff in between, and check at regular intervals. This makes for a better time management and focus. You will save time doing this.

Now you will also be able to find your emails, especially if your email client has a good search function.

Now, set expectations with clients and team members by establishing your preferred method of contact. For example, for all urgent matters I prefer to receive an sms or phone call. If it can wait 24 hours then I prefer email.

Once I set this expectation, I find that most people respect the system works and they use it, even clients.

My diary is set so that 95% of the time, I can clear my email first thing in the morning. I set aside an hour, unless it is campaign critical, then I may increase the time for email. It is always in the diary and I stay away from it in between.

I commit to returning phone calls as soon as possible, and encourage use of my voice mail. I prioritise my return calls, and gently, respectfully discourage team members from using the phone if it is not important.

Email mountains can eat our energy, and de-motivate us, we must ensure our email is a positive contributor and not a time eater. They can give us a great excuse not to be with a client.

I do not use pc based IM very liberally. I think it is an interesting tool for people who are at their desk all day, but I believe it really interrupts your own productivity. It is too easy to send a quick message and then to continue to add comments. A few minutes x 50 times a day is hours lost! I love it socially, but restrict usage in the workplace.

I encourage friends and family to contact me after 18.00 hours, or use my voicemail or personal email address. If it is urgent, then of course I want them to contact me. I just don't need to know that Aunt Nancy has decided to marry, or have a hip replacement in the middle of my work day – appropriate focus remember!

We want to create memorable human connections and the best way to do that is in person, the more remote the communication, the less it will work.

In the new generations, sms is becoming an accepted way of communicating, and I must say I love it, as it saves time. I do notice however, that it does not enhance that warm human connection we all need. The more we move into this virtual world, the more important human connection will become as a differentiator. No matter how cool technology is, we are still first and foremost human beings.

People are intrinsically becoming more isolated. They have trouble meeting and connecting to new friends or meeting their partners. Most people are social animals with a herding mentality, they still need the warmth of other humans to feel fulfilled. Never expect that this will really change, it is just a trend, and in the end human connection will win over e-connect as a sales habit!

Other daily traps to manage are:

The Corridor Snaggers, the people that want to stand with a coffee and just chat about things that are time wasting drivel. Bless them, they are social and often very nice, but they can rob you of valuable energy if entertained for too long. They are unlikely to be successful, or even very productive people!

The Meteorites, the people who always have something terrible, negative or dramatic to pass on, thus extracting some needed energy from every passer-by. Deflect the meteorites with charm and a smile, jolly them along with a positive statement and get the hell out of their way.

They Who Will Not Wait are the Senior Managers who expect you to drop everything, including your client, and run when they snap their fingers. Yet they are the same people who are getting agitated at quarter end, demanding to know why your deal is not yet closed! Actually, these leaders drive me nuts in a sales environment, it is obvious they do not understand the sales process, or they would not do this. Still, we have to manage them whilst still retaining our energy and motivation. This requires some extraordinary skill, however I do find they tend to forgive the Sales Legend for not being there every time, even though no one else is accorded such a privilege. Build your reputation as the Legend, the wolf, and I promise you will see a path through this.

The Hyenas, (see definition in Political Reference) best avoided but usually have to be tolerated. Generally, though they have thick hides, and can be easily placated by being allowed to float in and out pretending they are involved. You can manage them easily, by understanding their game and working with them. They are useful promoters of your legend, they are not a threat to a true Legend.

Desks Generally, I recommend to sales people that if you do not have a reason to sit at your desk, or in your own department then don't. This will of course depend on your company policy and Sales Leaders' requirements, however it is harder to stay motivated when parked at a desk in your own office.

Visit other departments, your client, work from home and focus on winning. Remember walk your talk as much as possible.

Many sales offices in large enterprises have introduced hot-desking for sales people, and it works very effectively. It changed expectations and perceptions of the sales people and the other internal staff. Sales people should be focussed on winning by building their networks and human connections, not distracted by the workings of the office.

Motivating The Mind

Motivating the mind and keeping it busy is an important contributor to staying upbeat and focussed on winning.

Our minds like to be busy, so if they are not occupied, boredom quickly sets in. Boredom is the enemy of a sales person. Boredom will consume energy at a rapid rate, and quickly convince your subconscious mind that the world around is dark. Dark matter also consumes energy faster than anything else in our Universe, and little is understood about why. What is known is that light and energy expand and grow, dark matter consumes that energy.

If you want to prove me wrong, go and sit in an unadorned, windowless room for 8 hours with nothing to do. At the end of that 8 hours sit down and write what you are thinking about and how you are feeling. You will be unique if you can prove me wrong! Even a high energy person, subjected to this experiment will emerge with an exhausted mind. That is why solitary confinement is used as a punishment.

A person wanting to retain energy needs to be kept busy. This does not mean you may not relax, but it means you have to ensure your mind remains in a positive occupied state.

Ideal ways to relax include massage, floatation, meditation. An hour of one of those techniques and you will feel almost as good as a short holiday break! This is because your mind is either busy relaxing ☺ or you have fallen calmly asleep.

It is not ideal for a high performance sales person to work 20 hours a day for a year, then go lie on a deserted beach for a week. The extremes are not really that good for your mind. Most Sales Legends

I know take short, interesting breaks whenever possible ensuring they enjoy their life. They do work hard, but not necessarily as long hours as you may expect. This is because, as we discussed earlier they are organised in their personal life, to allow maximum focus on their work.

Some time ago, I worked with a guy called Tim. We had the same sales role, but different territories of a similar type.

He was always working late, really long hours. My results were much better. He used to say he didn't know how I could do it, great results yet usually finished work by 18:30 most days.

Well, I decided to study his behaviour and work out the difference.

He had no focus between 0800 and 1800. he was sorting out problems in his personal life like unpaid bills, lost equipment needed by his kids for sport, all sorts of things. He gossiped, he was a corridor snagger, he liked to spend time internally focussed on what was happening within his company. He neglected sufficient client visits on the basis he needed to read his emails and be sure he was up to date with product changes.

Once most others had left the premises, he would begin to work on his proposals, respond to his clients emails, call people at home to show he was working late and he never left the office before 21:00, often 22:00!

He was tired, run down and his mind was busy with the problems of all his colleagues. He constantly complained about our leader, (who by the way was crap) and let it all build up on top of him. His office was a mess, and highly disorganised. He would spend sometimes half an hour looking for a document he put somewhere. He had committed his mind to failure and his energy was absorbed by dark stories from colleagues.

Let us look at ways to help your mind stay busy and motivated.

At Work:

First and foremost focus on winning increased business, and new clients if appropriate. This means keep yourself motivated by walking your talk, selling yourself and your clients internally, increasing your network of contacts with great human connections. Find out about new products and services from people in your organisation rather than an email. Nothing makes a new product or service come alive faster than someone who is passionate about it, an email is very flat from an energy perspective.

If you can share even small successes daily with many people, it energises you and motivates them!

Make new connections within your client base, and develop ideas for improving client business by using your products and services.

Spend every minute of every day moving forward.

Moving forward, and developing new clients, new contacts, new business. Always progressing toward your goals is a way to maintain high energy levels and not leaving your mind to welcome your enemy - boredom.

Away From Work:

This is an equally important time for you to maintain activity and states of mind that credit energy back to your bank. Remember we said earlier, focus on work at work, then focus on your family, hobby or sport in your free time.

There is an old saying 'If you want a job done, give it to a busy person!'

It is true, and whilst an idle mind creates trouble, a busy mind gets things done generating a sense of achievement and satisfaction.

So when you leave work, plan your next day. Unless there is a crisis, relegate your work to a secondary place in your mind.

You can then enhance the trip and listen to music that you love on the way home. Try and relax and use that time as quality time, you can even catch up on calls to friends and family, if your car has hands free of course!

I use this time to think about how things went, what I can improve on tomorrow, and plan the day ahead whilst listening to favourite music. I smile at other drivers, and often get a smile back. I do not stress about one minute less because someone took an out of turn, or found themselves in a wrong lane. I let them in with a smile.

If you listen to the radio, do not listen to every news bulletin being repeated, generally the news is bad news – if you know what you need to know, turn it off. I read my news on the internet, that way I may select what is relevant to me, and leave the rest to all the people who like to focus on, and repeat, the negative.

If you go by public transport then use your iPod, or even speak to someone else about their day, take one minute more for the person next to you. You will arrive home relaxed and ready to be an active, engaging, family member.

Try as much as possible to make time not actually working, to be quality time, it does a lot for your demeanour and your energy.

If you are going to miss your plane due to traffic, then you are going to miss your plane. A fact you cannot change. Instead of getting aggravated, start enacting your plan B, such as setting up a conference line, or changing the meeting time or date, or having someone else represent you. In the end getting stressed loses you energy, and as this is a situation you cannot change, you might as well do what you can in a positive way. Then redeploy the time to something positive, otherwise you will bear down upon yourself and deplete energy.

When you are home, try and spend quality time with your family. This is an age where people are permitted, even encouraged, to have lifestyle balance. Children are better off if they do not have to hear that Mum or Dad are too busy for them. If you play sport, give your attention and focus to improving and/or enjoying that sport. The same for your hobbies and interests, and do not forget your personal relationships, they are important.

The worst thing you can do, is go and sit in front of TV and watch whatever you can find. Sitting there flicking about the channels trying to find something to occupy your mind, is not relaxing it is a symptom of boredom. This is the archetypical behaviour of the masses, and not that of a Sales Legend.

Carefully select what you like to watch, and take care that you do not watch programs with lots of angst and misery, these are also for the masses, not for a potential Sales Legend!

If you have no family, no friends, no hobbies, sports or interests then you probably need a psychiatrist not me, and you are likely not yet destined to be a Sales Legend! The less you fill your life with, then the less you have in your mind with which to entertain yourself and others!

So pursue things that interest you, and enjoy your friends and family when you are not at work. Keep your mind occupied so it does not cause trouble!

If you are stressed, then I recommend using the common fast distress methods like spa treatments, swimming, massage, shiatsu therapy, and even meditation. Getting lost in a good book, or listening to an inspiring piece of music, time with a pet or a child, watch a sunset – all these things will help you distress faster.

Look for the best in everyone and everything.

A special technique for feeling happier and with more energy, is to appreciate every day, everything that you have in your life!

Actually do this, walk around your house and appreciate pieces of art, or a comfy sofa, or a nice coloured wall, or a nice flower you grew. These small random acts of kindness to ourselves are very motivational.

It is a great energy boost to start every day with the affirmation

'I appreciate everything I have every day. I am successful, healthy, happy, and I have what I need.'

This said every morning in the shower will have your energy soaring every morning after a couple of weeks – truly – try it!

Use every skill available to you in idle moments such as visualisation or your desired results, appreciation, affirmations, positive inputs – pictures, sounds, textures.

When I travel for my work, I always include some 'me time'. Maybe it is a few hours for a favourite store, or a wonderful place I want to see. Maybe it is adding a weekend to a three day business trip and seeing somewhere new.

Many colleagues have travelled the globe for business, but have rarely seen anything outside the office and the hotel room. If you like new places, faces, smells and tastes this is motivational, and refreshing break that rewards you.

Most of my colleagues rarely do this, they say they are too busy, and yet I achieve equal or better results!

I have seen places I would never have seen otherwise, and met people that have richly contributed to my life tapestry. It keeps me motivated!

For things that are important to you, take a few moments out of a day, at an appropriate time. This can also be rewarding.

> *I am under pressure to complete my draft, I know I am close to deadline.*

Today, someone I admire enormously was unfairly slammed by a media person who should know better. I took 30 minutes out, and I wrote a Letter to that Editor and tried to rectify an injustice.

It was important to me, I prioritised it in. One of my colleagues told me that it should have waited until I finished the book, but I said no it was blocking my energy and fighting injustice may not be postponed.

That 30 minute action has restored my energy, which took a battering when I discovered the damage, unfairly caused to this persons' reputation.

The following day, my energy received a huge boost when I discovered my efforts had been rewarded!

Make sure that your time is always spent, whether at work or play, with mind occupied with positive things.

Protecting your mind, and ensuring quality input, will accord you also better health.

Maintaining The Body

Now the body needs some sensible things to happen if you are to stay motivated, and achieving.

Your body needs proper food, when you are hungry. If you put garbage in your body consistently, then you will in the end get only garbage out.

To sustain peak levels of energy you need your body and mind in synch.

So if you are ensuring your mind is occupied with positive inputs, then ensure your body is to.

A decent balanced diet is essential to maintaining energy. I also recommend vitamin supplements to many of the people I am coaching because unless you grow your own fresh food, then what you buy from the supermarket has lost a lot of vitamin value by the time you eat it. I am not going to lecture intelligent people on what is a sensible balanced diet, you already know that, or you can find more than you need on this subject on the internet.

Vitamin supplements depend a bit on your own body needs, but in general be sure you are at least taking vitamin C at 1000mg a day to ward off all the viruses that float about. An executive B is good for stress levels, that's why they call it Executive B! I also usually recommend a Vitamin E and a Calcium Magnesium supplement. The rest depends on you, your diet, your stress levels and what your body type needs to stay in peak. Apart from energy, the other key reason to have a high vitamin intake is to boost your immune system to ensure you have the maximum number of days in which to pursue your dreams, goals and life plan.

Regular moderate exercise is essential, but normally as a sales executive you will get a lot of good walking, stair climbing, and fresh air every day as part of your active work life. Exercise is good, the level beyond an active life is up to your own preference and your doctors' advice.

Fresh air is essential, as is feeling the ground under your feet. Try and spend some time in a park, or a forest at least once a week. Touch the earth, and watch the trees never tire generating energy. Watch a bird, and remember that whilst they can fly they also have to hunt for food every single day to survive.

You can fly (metaphorically) and yet you have the privilege of just buying your food. What an advantage!

Rest is very important and frequently overlooked. You will know what level of sleep your body needs. A recommended level is normally 6 – 8 hours. I can function on 6 for awhile, but prefer 8. I have a colleague who never needs more than 6. Quality of rest is actually more important than the number of hours. Watch that last 30 minutes before you sleep, and try not to be watching something disturbing to your mind, stressful, or even that requires too much thought. That last half hour dictates the sort of sleep pattern you will likely have. Never go straight from work, or driving, or high activity levels straight to sleep for the night. Your brain will not rest properly. Take 30 minutes and shower, bath, relax, listen to some soft music – whatever – just do not run and drop. It is bad for your body.

If you are in the unfortunate position of needing to do 24-36 hours wrapping up a bid, and many of you have to do this from time to time, then take small breaks for quick naps in between. Find an office sofa, or be a hero and take in a blow up mattress for all to share throughout the night. If everyone can take 15-30 minutes rest every few hours, everything will go smoother, less mistakes and better maintenance of energy levels. Supply a bowl of high energy fruits for the team, instead of colas, coffee and pizzas.

Avoid excess of everything! Excess of some good things, can also be harmful. Everything should be in balance, so best to avoid any abuse or excess, in your pursuit of success.

Protecting your body is protecting your immune system. Protecting your immune system means higher personal productivity potential. This of course means higher levels of achievement and satisfaction.

Remember to actively seek out, and take, those short 'me' breaks so that you remain free of resentment, and full of positive energy.

Bad Weather Tips

So, despite all you did, you have crashed – How do you get your energy back?

First, reread the above coaching. What did you neglect to do? If you say 'Nothing', I am sorry but I do not believe you!

You forgot something, maybe you thought it didn't matter, but it obviously did.

It just is not that hard, to stay motivated, if you take care of the inputs to body and mind, and stay true to your integrity.

Sometimes we allow other people to lead us in our life, we choose to allow them to take our energy every day.

If your job is not challenging, why not? Is it that you have done everything you can, and your company does not allow you to have a new opportunity? Or are you your own limiting factor?

Is there a personal situation that is draining your energy? If so, this must be addressed and a solution found, before you go down under too heavy a load. Too many citizens of Earth are carrying around heavy sacks of bricks, that they could leave behind, metaphorically speaking.

You need to have a sales role with unlimited potential, or else success will bring you to a flat point.

It is easy to see this burn out if we allow ourselves to get bored. This is often our own fault, we stop doing what made us successful in the first place, or we have reached certain levels and think now what?

Go and get yourself fired up for more, or if someone will not let you, then get out and find a company that will!

Sometimes, I have done a job well, so well that I know I could take a holiday for a month and still make target because I have a great team. Then I feel I have outgrown the role, so I ask for another, or I move onto a new challenge! I do not let the darkness of boredom to set in! The price is too high for me.

Sea changes only work if you know that you really want to do something else! They do not work if chosen because you are sick of what you do. A high achiever will need to be a high achiever in any chosen field. Even if you choose to do social work, you will find yourself setting your own goals and trying to achieve miracles! You may be more frustrated than ever, because you will be surrounded by people who are not motivated by the same rewards as you, they have a valuable but different set of goals. You may have been able to contribute more by selling more, earning more and giving a huge chunk to the same social cause!

Get my drift? Unless you are equally passionate about what you want to do next, it rarely works to go open a bar on a beach to get away from it all. It is, however ok to fantasise about it for mind breaks ☺ Truth is that bar will drive you nuts within a few months, unless being a bar owner is something you feel very passionate about! To test yourself, go work in a bar for a month for no pay to learn, then decide.

So when your mental, or physical weather is bad, you need to spend time to re-motivate yourself.

First you need to do some research on what exactly is the problem. Maybe you just need constant change, maybe you hate your boss, maybe you are just sick of the same people every day. You need to identify what is wrong.

In 90% of cases I see like this, as a coach, I find that the bad weather is due to not enough 'me' time. Too much excess makes us unhappy, too much excess of anything. Most of us are not obsessed, we need variety, change and challenge. So we need to ensure we have rewarded 'us' enough every day, week, and year!

> *One of the best sales people I ever hired was a passionate fisherman. His favourite thing in life was to heli-fish. They fly you out to some rock in the middle of the ocean, lower you and your gear onto a rock, and come back and get you a few hours later. Not my idea of fun, but it was his.*
>
> *We came to an agreement. He did not like to take time out from his family on the weekend to do this, as he had young kids and felt it was too selfish. So he became bored and restless at work, because he couldn't heli-fish.*
>
> *The agreement was – in any month he achieved 120% or better, he could take a work day and go heli-fishing.*
>
> *He never missed his 120%, he was highly motivated to the point of once wearing out a patch of my carpet in the close of a huge deal! It cost me 12 extra days off, but it paid back*

> *in outstanding productivity and he remained a ball of energy that also motivated others in the team.*

Burn out is mostly lack of self reward in the way of 'me' time. High achievers must have a few minutes, or hours, or even days here and there to do things they really want to do. This may involve friends and family, it may not, but it sure does not involve work!

It may not even involve work time, it just needs to be that through all your hard work, stress and sometimes difficult clients or colleagues, you have the reward of doing things you personally really love to do!

Ensure that you relax and enjoy quality time with family, friends, your hobbies, and interests. Pamper yourself regularly with a spa treatment that works for you, or a nice bottle of wine, or your favourite meal. Take walks in the fresh air and if possible in a location you love such as the sea, the desert, the evening, the forest. Stop and take a few minutes to watch more sunsets, or sunrises; to look at a rainbow; to observe wildlife beside the highway; or to visit places of interest. If you maintain a quality lifestyle balance you will be more productive, achieve better results, be more engaging and be happy in yourself. You are unlikely to burn out.

If you need organising personally then buy *'30 Days of Inspiration'* I wrote this specifically for you. It is a simple day by day guide to setting up your life to be in a balanced lifestyle with time for success!

If you find that no matter what you do, you can't seem to feel happy, then read and action the ARPIFEE program in The Little Red Success Book.

It is the guide I wrote after being told that living in a state of euphoria was a problem ☺

I realised so few people were actually really happy that I was a bit of a weirdo, so I better try and tell people about how to sort out why they are unhappy and fix it!

If you are really, intrinsically happy then it is hard to burn out!

That was my plug for my two previous books, but in fairness, they are relevant here and may just help one of you out on an aspect of your lifestyle balance you need coaching on.

What next?

Go out and fly!

Take the time and deploy your energy to make extraordinary human connections, by listening actively, engaging people in the moment, and delivering relevant, interesting messages.

Stay in your integrity and respect everyone with whom you come into contact. Give everyone you meet just one minute more and increase your network of people who wish you well, thus giving you energy. Appreciate what you have, and thank everyone for what you are given be that time, power, money, introduction or anything else, even a lesson you needed to learn.

Qualify your leads fully, and commit to those you know you can win. Then plan creative strategies, and implement them with confidence and passion by walking your talk, leading and motivating those around you. Focus on winning, and follow up everyone involved every day. Take total responsibility, and if you lose a deal, then blame no one but yourself.

Stay alert to your political references but rarely, if ever, engage. Protect your reputation and let no one have cause to damage it because of a moment of stupidity.

Last, but not least, avoid allowing your ego to control your actions, and reactions. Instead have faith in the light of your own integrity and reputation. Use the Law of Attraction, rather than ignore it, and enjoy a life with more abundance of the things that really matter to you.

Be a luminary, someone who attracts who and what they need, when they need them, like moths to a flame.

If you do these things you will have enthusiastic customers, absolutely delighted by your sales campaigns, and committed to your success.

You will be in the top percentile of your profession, you will be a 999er and maybe you will also be a Legend!

On a personal level watch more sunsets, hear more great pieces of music, watch fabulous movies, hug and play with your family and friends, laugh a lot and be unafraid to try something new!

Life is a great adventure, and your income as a top sales person allows you to enjoy whatever you want, you are privileged to have this knowledge, this potential. Remember to appreciate everything you have every day!

I wish you Great Selling and a Happy Life!

Look famous

Be Legendary

Appear Complex

Act Easy

Radiate Presence

Travel Light

Seem a Dream

Prove Real

Source:

Our Office Wall. Author Unknown. ..Well Loved and Read Often By Many!

It perfectly captures the enigmatic charisma of a Sales Legend!

MORE INFORMATION

999 LEGENDARY SELLING FOR THE 21ST CENTURY

Available as a Three Day Sales Training and Coaching Programme.

Company Benefits include:

- 999 helps your sales force forecast more accurately and win more consistently.
- 999 is a sales coaching program with measurable Return on Investment.
- 999 is generic, and therefore enhances your existing investment in CRM, operational methodologies and systems.
- 999 maximises results from resource deployment, minimizing cost of sales.
- 999 coaching can increase your revenue and improve margins

999 The Corporate Sales Training and Coaching Programme
Designed and Delivered Globally by 360plus5

360plus5 provides a coaching and training experience that is practically unique in the market place today. The people who lead the custom built sessions and programmes are not typical trainers. Each and every one of the Fellows that work with 360plus5 are seasoned, C-Level experts that have served their time in the field in a leading role. Our unique business model allows them to efficiently deliver their services to companies all over the world.

Customers Include:

BT, KPN Telecom, Infonet, Fidelity, Commodore, Hybris, Logica, Business Objects, Austria Telekom, Space Hellas, PeopleSoft, Keane,

IBM, Miyowa, Cognos, Hyperion, Memex, Unic, Dade Behring, Global Knowledge.

The coaching sessions are typically organised into three sections. The first is a media led overview delivered by an expert in the subject. These modules in the close coaching format have duration of between 30 minutes and one hour. They are designed to be interactive and to get the feedback and ideas of the delegates.

Most of the modules have a targeted workshop where the delegates have a set of tasks that are designed to reinforce and interpret the material within the first section.

Finally, an interactive discussion and note taking session is hosted by the expert so that the material and knowledge can be examined in relation directly to the company's needs and working environment.

The Key Modules include:

| Integrity | Follow Up | Human Connection | Strategy |

| Political Reference | Customer Enthusiasm | Focus |

| Hard Line Qualification | Networking & Reputation | The Consortium |

For more information please contact us:

999@360plus5.com

terrie.anderson@easyonlineportals.com

Europe +31 235490031 or +44 208 1339828

APAC +61 408180854   **USA** +1 858303890

999 Legendary Selling – The Corporate Sales Training Program

999 Legendary Selling for the 21st Century

Keynotes

Terrie Anderson is available for motivational and sales keynote engagements worldwide.

Inspire your sales team, partner organisation or group with a highly energetic, passionate and dynamic keynote address from this charismatic, proven sales leader and accomplished author.

Consultancy

If your sales organisation is flagging, needs a shot in the arm or has a high level opportunity that you want to win, then please send us an email or call us. We will be delighted to assist however we can.

Terrie is also available for events for clients, management reviews, or Board Advisory services.

Coaching

Terrie Anderson provides coaching services online, and in person. She specialises in Sales, Sales Leadership and C Level Leadership personal coaching. We will be delighted to work with you to design a specially tailored program that provides the benefits and outcomes you are looking for.

Dynamic Coaching Days are also available for organisations, details on request.

Other Services

Directly, and through partnership we can assist you with most management, leadership and sales issues including industry leading psychometric testing and e-profiling; Executive Search and Interim Management; Coaching in Senior Candidate Selection and more.....

Contact Details for Terrie Anderson

Email:

terrie.anderson@easyonlineportals.com

Phone:

Your call is very welcome anytime:

Europe	+32 478 322335
UK	+44 208 1339828
USA	+1 415 8303890
NL	+31 23 549 0031
Australia	+61 7 31023890
	+61 408 180854

Websites:

www.999thelegend.com

www.terrieanderson.com

www.trulygreatleadership.com

www.360plus5.com

Other Books By Terrie Anderson

30 Days of Inspiration is a Guide to Personal Fulfilment.

It is possible to adapt your lifestyle into one that attracts success into your life.

It does not matter if you are feeling de-motivated today, you can choose to change your mind set and take control of your life in just one month.

Ideal book to help you organise your life and have more time.

This is a beginning, a way to understand what you want and where you want to go, then guide you how to get there.

30 Days of Inspiration can help you:

Realise Your Personal Potential

Achieve Your Goals

Improve Your Image and Self Esteem

Take Control of Your Life

Fast Track Your Career

Have More Time For Yourself

Improve Communication

Enhance Relationships

You can buy this book online or order via your local bookstore by quoting **ISBN 978-0980724806**

The Little Red Success Book

How To Achieve Whatever You Want Out Of Life

Do you want to really understand the Laws of Attraction and Abundance?

The LITTLE RED SUCCESS BOOK is only the beginning. Its purpose is to inspire you to enter on a quest, with rewards potentially more wonderful than you have ever believed possible.

Seven simple steps, guiding you on a path to achieving what you want out of life, are easily and logically explained. It is easy to read and simple to follow. You will feel that the author is actually speaking to you directly.

First published in 1994, now updated, this book has helped many people achieve their dreams.

The ideal book for anyone just starting out on a quest for a better life, success in business or the fulfilment of any dream.

Practical advice that is also equally applicable in building business and career development, as it is in personal development.

You can buy this book online or order via your local bookstore by quoting **ISBN 978-0473025854**

360PLUS5
A FELLOWSHIP

360plus5 has invited some of the most experienced executives available throughout the world to be Fellows. The selection process was conducted by finding C-Level people who have more than 20 years experience. They are all proven entrepreneurs who have a track record of outstanding achievement and success.

Fellows are articulate and well known within their chosen field of knowledge. They have an excellent network of colleagues and call upon real life experience to deliver their insights into improving your business.

Coaching from these people is interesting, engaging and above all is the best way to learn new techniques.

A wide variety of specialist and general coaching programmes have been developed in conjunction with 360plus5's Fellows. The subjects are based upon the skills and expertise that is on offer from them.

Contact us: 999@360plus5.com

Phone: +31 23 549 0031

www.360plus5.com

www.ingramcontent.com/pod-product-compliance
Lightning Source LLC
Chambersburg PA
CBHW081915180426
43198CB00038B/2642